First Century Methods I:

Recovering Ancient Methods of Bible Study

Dr. Anne Davis

BibleInteract
RECOVERING ANCIENT METHODS OF BIBLE STUDY

Published by BibleInteract, Inc.
ISBN-13: 978-1495281389
ISBN-10: 1495281388

Cover design by Faith A. Benson

BibleInteract
865 Los Pueblos Street
Los Alamos, NM 87544

www.bibleinteract.com

TABLE OF CONTENTS

Introduction
Getting Started and Suggestions for Group Leaders

Are you ready for a startling statistic? There are approximately 41,000 Christian denominations and organizations in the world.[1] Many of them profess a creed, which is a statement of belief to which members must adhere in order to belong and participate. "Why," we ask, "are Christians unable to agree on what the Bible says?"

All of us are born with a curious nature. We know that small children constantly demand "What is this? What is that? Why...? How...?" Yet the world (through our history and culture) has done a remarkable job of driving this curiosity out of us. You are probably no longer asking, "What is this? What is that? Why and how?" I have found that the field of religion is especially adept at replacing natural curiosity with acceptance and belief. So, Christians tend to join the church that makes them most comfortable.

As an adult, I am still naturally curious. I sometimes picture myself as Curious George, the adorable little monkey of childhood memory whose curiosity stimulates learning even though his actions are perceived by the world as mischief. I have concluded that my curiosity is a blessing, and I am reassured by a wonderful verse in the Gospel of Matthew. "Truly I say to you, unless you are converted [changed] and become like children, you will not enter the kingdom of heaven" (Mat 18:3).

My training has been in New Testament theology, but I never stopped questioning what I was being taught, especially if it made no sense to me. My natural curiosity led me to examine and compare modern methods of Bible study with the way people at the time of Yeshua perceived the Holy Writings and the manner in which they searched for answers to questions about their lives and their God. There is an ample amount of literature, both Jewish and Christian, from this period of time, which became the focus of my investigation. This work led me to recover ancient methods of searching the Scriptures, which turned out to be very different from our modern methods of Bible study.

Required Resources

- You will, of course, need a Bible. Dr. Davis will be reading from the New American Standard Bible (NASB), but you can use another Bible version if you wish.

- You will also need a Bible atlas that includes information about both geography and history of ancient Israel. If you do not already have a Bible atlas, we suggest *Holman Bible Atlas* by Thomas V. Brisco.

- One other required resource is a good book on the customs and manners of ancient Israel. If you do not already have such a book, we recommend *Manners & Customs in the Bible* by Victor H. Matthews.

---

[1] This statistic was published in a 2010 study conducted by the Center for the Study of Global Christianity (CSGC) at Gordon-Conwell Theological Seminary. Although there is some overlapping due to cultural distinctions in different countries, their conclusion demands thoughtful attention.

Video Lectures

There are twelve video lectures on three DVD discs that accompany this workbook, one lecture for each chapter. Each lecture is approximately 28-1/2 minutes long. In the first half of the program (Chapters 1-6) you will be working exclusively in the Hebrew Scriptures. In Chapters 7-8 the focus will be on the New Testament. However, the New Testament often cites and refers to the Hebrew Scriptures, so in the second half of the program the two testaments will come together as one unified message.

Required Memorization of the Hebrew and Greek Alphabets

For the first six chapters you will need to learn the Hebrew alphabet because you will be working with original words in the Hebrew Scriptures. The purpose of the program is not to teach the biblical language. Instead, you will only be working with individual words. For Chapters 7-12 you will need to learn the biblical Greek alphabet so you can work with Greek New Testament Words. You will find instruction for learning these alphabets on the BibleInteract website.

Note to Group Leaders

You will undoubtedly find this course filled with new information that will be challenging and provocative. As a teacher or group leader, you will need to review the entire program first, both the lectures and the workbook. Your role will then become one of guiding and facilitating. You will begin by selecting which exercises are appropriate for your group. We have tried to include activities that are for beginning, intermediate and advanced levels. Do not feel obligated to do everything in the workbook but be selective. You will then be promoting lively discussion, stimulating incisive questions, and encouraging a search in the Scriptures for meaningful answers. If your group has a question, don't let them depend on you for the answer. Guide them to discover their own answer.

Let me make a comment on the name of God's son. I have used the name Yeshua because the focus is to encourage you to think with a first century Hebraic mind. However, you should use the name that is most comfortable to your group. If they prefer the name Jesus, then that is the name that you should use.

The Workbook

Each chapter of the Workbook contains seven parts.

1. First, before watching the video lecture, you should carefully consider the brief Summary, which will give you a focus on what to expect in the lecture.

2. Next you will be watching the video lecture. The workbook includes an outline of this lecture, and we encourage you to take notes as you listen. The purpose of the outline is to encourage organized thought that will facilitate later discussion.

3. After listening to the lecture, there are Words to be Defined, which should not take much time to complete unless part of the lecture needs further explanation.

4. Questions for Comprehension will assess how well you understood the lecture, and will reinforce what you have just heard.

5. Next comes the heart of the program, which is called Building Skills. This section is an essential element and should never be skipped, although the leader may decide to tackle only one exercise for a group activity. Learning how to use first century methods, which uncover a depth of meaning, is a skill, and all skills require practice.

6. Questions for Discussion is another important part of the program. The group leader will guide participants away from a tendency to look for a black-and-white answer. Therefore, the workbook asks questions, the group leader should pose questions, and members of the group should learn to ask their own questions. Then the group should explore together how to find answers to these questions. Feel free to create and add your own Questions for Discussion. In fact, the leader might ask members of the group to compose one or more of their own questions before coming together in discussion.

7. Application Questions encourage practical use of what you have learned. Again, feel free to create your own application questions.

Challenge Yourself!

Throughout the workbook, you will see these "Challenge Yourself" sections. These questions are more advanced and are not required for beginner- or intermediate-level students, but don't be afraid to try to answer them anyway.

Leading a Discussion

By presenting a new perspective on approaching and studying the Scriptures, I have chosen to intentionally encourage questions that lead not to definitive answers from the group leader but to provocative discussion in the group. Participants should eventually feel comfortable disputing the interpretive suggestions in the lecture, and even of the group leader and other students. However, a discussion leader should guide members of the group to follow two important requirements.

First, you should clearly and briefly state your main idea, which must then be followed by supporting evidence. Second, the discussion leader should encourage participants to speak in a compassionate manner. The modern literary term for this rhetorical skill is "couching," which evokes a visual image of a psychiatrist speaking compassionately to a patient on the couch. The good doctor wishes his or her patient to confront some aspect of thinking that might best be changed to a more advantageous perspective. The group should likewise avoid direct confrontation, and should avoid being judgmental. Instead, mimic the psychiatrist who gently employs couching terms.

- "Have you ever considered...?"
- "Perhaps there might be another possibility..."
- "For the sake of discussion, let us look at..."
- "I used to think that too, but now..."
- "There might be another way of approaching this verse..."

Sample Schedule

There are twelve chapters, and we recommend you allocate two hours for each chapter. You may decide to spend more time if you wish, but two hours per chapter is the norm.

If your group meets one hour each week, we suggest you show the video in the first half hour followed by the second half hour of discussion. You will then need another hour in the following week to complete the work for that chapter. Of course, if your group meets for more than one hour each week, you will likely complete one chapter each week.

As an alternative, you may wish to have members watch the video at home before coming together for the group discussion. This approach allows participants to watch the video more than once. Certain exercises can also be completed at home such as Words to be Defined and Questions for Comprehension. However, the remaining sections of the workbook, Building Skills, Questions for Discussion and Application Questions, are best accomplished through group discussion.

SAMPLE SCHEDULE

Session	Dates	Topic
Learn the Hebrew Alphabet		
1	Weeks 1 & 2	Comparing Hebrew and Greek Thought
2	Weeks 3 & 4	Importance of History, Geography and Culture
3	Weeks 5 & 6	Mysterious Artistry of Biblical Poetry
4	Weeks 7 & 8	Context and Key Words
5	Weeks 9 & 10	Imagery, Symbolism and Metaphors
6	Weeks 11 & 12	Symbolism of Names and Numbers
Learn the Greek Alphabet		
7	Weeks 13 & 14	Echoes and Commentary
8	Weeks 15 & 16	Word Study and Patterns
9	Weeks 17 & 18	Penetrating a Chiastic Construction
10	Weeks 19 & 20	What to do with a Citation
11	Weeks 21 & 22	Connecting the Two Testaments
12	Weeks 23 & 24	Stewards of the Mysteries of God

Support from BibleInteract

- If you would like additional workbooks or DVDs, you may contact BibleInteract.

- Students in a Degree or Certification program with The Bible Learning University, an online educational program operated by BibleInteract, will have an Advisor to whom they may turn for help.

- If you are the leader of a group that is using this material, you may register with BibleInteract, which will allow you to receive help as needed. BibleInteract will send the registered leader a Teacher's Manual.

BibleInteract, Inc., 865 Los Pueblos Street, Los Alamos, NM 87544
info@bibleinteract.com ▪ (505) 620-3842
http://bibleinteract.com ▪ http://bibleinteract.tv

Chapter 1
Comparing Hebrew and Greek Thought

Summary

You will begin by identifying your Greek, western tradition of Bible study in order to compare it with the first century Hebraic approach. This chapter will give you four characteristics of the Hebraic approach with examples from Scripture.

Outline of Lecture

Below is an outline of the video lecture. We suggest that you take brief notes in the space provided as you watch the lecture. The purpose of the outline is to promote organization of thought.

I.   Introduction

   A.   Goals of the course

   B.   Bible versions

   C.   Memorize alphabets

   D.   Chapter 1 overview

II.   How do we study the Bible today

   A.   Hermeneutics

   B.   Theology

III.   Four Hebraic principles

   A.   Stretch for the truth

      1.   Compare Greek and Hebrew

      2.   Ask questions, discuss and dialogue, search the Scriptures

      3.   Example: Mat 19:3-8 (debating Dt 24:1-4 and the concept of divorce)

         a.   Ancient culture – Pharisees and Sadducees

         b.   "Have you not read…." - irony

         c.   Two citations – Gen 1:27; 2:24

         d.   Irony directed against the Pharisees about their hardness of heart

     e.   Two citations – Deut 24:1-4; Jer 3:1, 12-14

     f.   Deeper meaning – in the beginning God was one with mankind, and man and his wife were also together as one.

   B.   Be like the master

    1. Living out the words he speaks

    2. Example – Mat 10:24-25

   C.   Uncover mysteries

    1. Greek

     1. Literal interpretation

     2. Figures of speech

     3. Theology – let others tell you what it means

    2. Hebraic

     a. God is the author

     b. *p'shat*

     c. *midrash*

    3.   Example: Mat 13:11

   D.   Listen for anything unusual

    1. Example – Gal 2:16

     1.   Listen to the repetitions

     2.   You will be learning how to understand the deeper meaning from the repetitions and other linguistic devices that the ancient ear would have heard

Words to be Defined

1. Hermeneutics_____

_____

_____

2. Theology_____

_____

_____

3. *P'shat*_____

_____

_____

4. *Midrash*_____

_____

_____

Questions for Comprehension

1. What are the four characteristics of thinking Hebraically? Explain each one._____

_____

_____

_____

_____

_____

2. What is the difference between a Greek teacher and a Hebrew teacher?_____

_____

_____

_____

_____

_____

3. Compare the Greek way of perceiving truth in Scripture with the Hebraic way of perceiving truth in Scripture?_____

_____

_____

_____

_____

_____

_____

_____

4. How did the children in ancient Israel learn the Scriptures?_____

_____

_____

5. Describe the irony that Yeshua used in Matthew 19:3-8._____

_____

_____

_____

_____

_____

_____

_____

Building Skills

You must memorize the Hebrew alphabet. You will find video instruction on the BibleInteract website: http://bibleinteract.com

Questions for Discussion

1. How hard is it for you to ask questions about a passage in the Bible? How hard is it to ask questions about what you have been taught?_____

    _____

    _____

    _____

    _____

2. How would you describe the interaction of Yeshua with the Pharisees in Matthew 19:3-11? Was it a discussion? Was it a dialogue? Was it a debate? Or what was it? How was this interaction different from a modern classroom today?_____

    _____

    _____

    _____

    _____

    _____

    _____

    _____

    _____

3. The members of your group are probably using different Bible versions. Consider the information in letters a-d below. Then compare your different translations of Psalm 4:2 and Hebrews 1:3.

   1. The King James Version (KJV) translates closely to the original text. However, it uses archaic words like "thee" and "thou."

   2. The New International Version (NIV) takes liberties with the translation in order to make it easier to understand. However, this process of translation leads to a tendency toward interpretation of the text.

   3. The New American Standard Bible (NASB), like the KJV, translates as closely to the original as possible while, at the same time, using more contemporary words.

   4. A Reference Bible has notes in the middle or bottom margins.

Psalm 4:2 (NASB)	Psalm 4:2 (KJV)	Psalm 4:2 (NIV)
O sons of men, how long will my honor become a reproach? *How long* will you love what is worthless and aim at deception? Selah.	O ye sons of men, how long will ye turn my glory into shame? how long will ye love vanity, and seek after leasing? Selah.	How long will you people turn my glory into shame? How long will you love delusions and seek false gods?
Hebrews 1:3 (NASB)	**Hebrews 1:3 (KJV)**	**Hebrews 1:3 (NIV)**
[3] And He is the radiance of His glory and the exact representation of His nature, and upholds all things by the word of His power. When He had made purification of sins, He sat down at the right hand of the Majesty on high,	[3] Who being the brightness of his glory, and the express image of his person, and upholding all things by the word of his power, when he had by himself purged our sins, sat down on the right hand of the Majesty on high:	[3] The Son is the radiance of God's glory and the exact representation of his being, sustaining all things by his powerful word. After he had provided purification for sins, he sat down at the right hand of the Majesty in heaven.

How does each translation lead to an interpretive meaning?

_____

_____

_____

_____

_____

_____

_____

In Matthew 19:3-11 Yeshua uses halachic midrash to respond to the Pharisees' accusing question about divorce. Halachic midrash finds two verses that are legally and conceptually similar and finds a relationship between them.

1. How were the Pharisees "testing" Yeshua?_____
   _____

2. How are the two verses below legally and conceptually similar?_____
   _____
   _____

   CITATION IN CAPITAL LETTERS:

   He who created them from the beginning MADE THEM MALE AND FEMALE.
   (Mat 19:4 citing Gen 1:27)

   CITATION IN CAPITAL LETTERS:

   FOR THIS REASON A MAN SHALL LEAVE HIS FATHER AND MOTHER AND BE JOINED TO HIS WIFE, AND THE TWO SHALL BECOME ONE FLESH '? (Mat 19:5 citing Gen 2:24)

3. How do these two verses lead to this conclusion: *"In the beginning there was no separation between God and mankind and also between husband and wife?"*_____
   _____

4. How are the next two verses below legally and conceptually similar?_____
   _____

   CITATION IN CAPITAL LETTERS:

   Why then did Moses command to GIVE HER A CERTIFICATE OF DIVORCE AND SEND her AWAY? (Mat 19:7 citing Deut 24:1-4)

   ALLUSION TO JEREMIAH:

   Because of your hardness of heart Moses permitted you to divorce your wives; but from the beginning it has not been this way. (Mat 19:8 alluding to Jer 3:1, 12-14)

5. How do these two verses lead this conclusion: *"God allows divorce, which is separation, because mankind is currently in a sinful condition. However, God is in the process of leading us back to the beginning when there was no separation."*_____
   _____

6. What is irony, and how is the following verse ironic?_____
   _____
   _____

   "Because of your hardness of heart Moses permitted you to divorce your wives; but from the beginning it has not been this way." Matthew 19:8

Application Questions

1. Dr. Davis encourages you to ask questions about the biblical text and also about what you have been taught. Without asking questions you will always be relying on the interpretation of others. However, learning to ask questions will help you penetrate a deeper understanding. How difficult will this be for you? Explain your answer. Try asking questions now (you will be learning in this course how to answer your questions)._____

_____

_____

_____

_____

_____

_____

_____

_____

_____

_____

_____

_____

2. In your traditional Bible study before starting this program, have you perceived the Pharisees as obstructing the teaching of Yeshua? Dr. Davis offered a different perspective. Irony was an acceptable method of teaching in the ancient world. With this understanding, revisit the following passages to see if your perspective of the Pharisees will change. Write your observations below.

Mat 3:5-9
Mat 12:1-7
Luke 5:17-26

_____

_____

_____

_____

_____

_____

_____

_____

_____

_____

Chapter 1 Quiz

1. Hermeneutics is a method of Bible study based on rules of interpretation, whereas the Hebraic approach "listens" to the text for anything unusual that might act as a clue leading to deeper meaning.
   a. True
   b. False

2. The western approach elevates the Bible as the Word of God whereas the Hebraic approach elevates the teacher who has a knowledge of its meaning.
   a. True
   b. False

3. We must not question our teacher, but we must "believe" what we are being taught.
   a. True
   b. False

4. According to the Hebraic approach, the study of Scripture is best conducted in pairs or in small group discussion.
   a. True
   b. False

5. How did Yeshua conduct his discussion with the Pharisees about divorce in Matthew 18:3-11?
   a. He used a figure of speech called irony.
   b. He used a figure of speech called hyperbole.
   c. He judged them as unholy.
   d. He condemned them as unbelievers.

6. An outstanding master or teacher talks the walk.
   a. True
   b. False

7. People in first century Israel believed there were mysteries in Scripture.
   a. True
   b. False

8. If we work to uncover a depth of meaning from Scripture using Hebraic methods, the unfortunate result is that we can make Scripture mean anything we want it to mean.
   a. True
   b. False

9. Both Christianity and Judaism agree that Scripture contains spiritual truths. However, how do they differ in their approach to uncover those truths?
    a. One has rules of interpretation and the other depends on the words of Yeshua.
    b. One elevates the teacher and the other elevates the minister.
    c. Christianity promotes listening with your heart whereas the Hebraic approach emphasizes reading the Torah.
    d. The role of the teacher in Christianity is to be well instructed in the meaning of Scripture whereas the role of the teacher according to the Hebraic approach is to walk in the ways of God.

10. How do we know we are walking in righteousness?
    a. We know the Word of God.
    b. We bear fruit by walking in the ways of God.
    c. We refrain from idleness.
    d. We are blames and without blemish.

Chapter 2
Importance of History, Geography and Culture

Summary

In this chapter, we can only introduce you to the critical importance of knowing the history, geography and culture of ancient Israel. You will have to pursue further study on your own. However, this chapter will give you suggestions of good reference material and a brief opportunity to practice using them.

Outline of Lecture

I.   Select a good Bible atlas that gives both the history and geography of ancient Israel

II.   Example of geography

    A. Divided kingdom of Israel

    B. Location: on the trade route between the two power centers of the ancient world

    c. Assyrians approach on their way to conquer Egypt

III. Example of history

    E. 2 Kings 15:29

        1. Location of Hazor, Gilead, Galilee, land of Naphtali

        2. Samaria, capital of the northern kingdom of Israel

    F. Ten lost tribes

        1. Taken into captivity by Assyria

        2. Distributed all around the Assyrian Empire

    G. God's miraculous rescue of Judah and Benjamin

        4. King Hezekiah

        5. 2 Kings 18:4-7, 13

        6. 2 Kings 18:31

        7. Hezekiah's prayer to God

        8. God's miracle – 2 Kings 19:35

IV.   Example of Culture – Mark 4:25-34

A. First tried all worldly remedies

B. Impurity – women separated during their monthly cycle

C. Respect of women for men – Luke 7:38

D. Ancient belief that power could pass from one to another by physical contact

E. Recommend *Manners and Customs in the Bible* by Victor Matthews

Words to be Defined

1. United and Divided Kingdoms_____
   _____
   _____
   _____

2. Mesopotamia_____
   _____
   _____
   _____

3. Ten Lost Tribes_____
   _____
   _____
   _____

4. Hezekiah_____
   _____
   _____
   _____

Questions for Comprehension

1. Who was the first king of Israel? Did he create a United Kingdom of the twelve tribes? Explain your answer. _____
   _____
   _____

2. Who was the last king of the United Kingdom? Describe the Divided Kingdom that followed, its locations and capitals._____
   _____
   _____
   _____

3. Who was Hezekiah? What is his importance in the biblical narrative?_____

_____

_____

_____

_____

4. What happened to the 10 northern tribes of Israel? What were the two southern tribes and how did they escape captivity by the Assyrians?_____

_____

_____

_____

_____

5. What are two reasons for the woman with an issue of blood having to stand at the outer edge of the crowd surrounding Yeshua?_____

_____

_____

_____

_____

Building Skills

1. Use the map on the next page to answer the following questions.

   a. Each of the 12 tribes was allocated an area for settlement. Match the name of the tribe to the corresponding number on your map.

   a. _____   g. _____

   b. _____   h. _____

   c. _____   i. _____

   d. _____   j. _____

   e. _____   k. _____

   f. _____   l. _____

   b. Circle on your map the surrounding enemies.

   c. The Philistines were one of these enemies, but they do not appear on your map. Use a Bible atlas to locate the Philistines and write their location on your map.

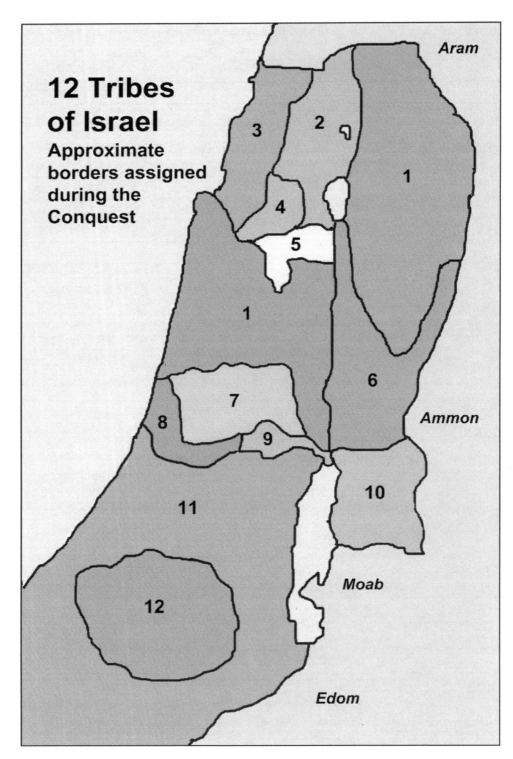

12 Tribes of Israel
Approximate borders assigned during the Conquest

2. Read the following verses *in their context* (context means the surrounding passage that gives each verse its meaning).

   a. Judges 3:9

b. Judges 3:15

c. Judges 4:3

d. Judges 6:6-7

e. Judges 10:10

Describe the Period of the Judges including its beginning and how it ended._____

_____

_____

_____

_____

_____

_____

Challenge Yourself!

Read Judges 3:15-30 about the story of Ehud and King Eglon. Use the map provided above to answer the following questions:

1. To understand the geography of the story, circle the following on the map:
   a. Tribe of Benjamin
   b. Moab

2. Mark the ford over the Jordan River at Jericho.

3. Mark the most likely route on your map from the tribe of Benjamin to Dibon, the capital of Moab.

4. We read that Ehud "turned away from the idols at Gilgal" (my translation from the Hebrew). Find Gilgal and mark it on your map.

5. The Moabites were occupying the land allocated by God to Reuben. Why do you think the tribe of Reuben had been unable to conquer this territory?_____

_____

_____

_____

_____

_____

_____

_____

_____

Questions for Discussion

1. Read the story of Ehud in Judges 3:15-30. Then answer the following:

   a. In Scripture, God's right hand signifies His power and His righteousness, which is why Yeshua is seated at His right hand. Therefore, it was considered a curse if a person was left-handed. Even in our own culture, until recent times, left-handed children were forced to write with their right hands. How does the fact that Ehud was left-handed cause irony in the story?_____

   _____

   _____

   _____

   _____

   _____

   b. In Judges 3:15, how is the manner of delivering tribute to the Moabites ironic?_____

   _____

   _____

   _____

   _____

   _____

   c. How did Ehud's left-handedness help him kill Eglon, King of Moab? How is this part of the story ironic?

   _____

   _____

   _____

   _____

   _____

   d. What smell do you think was coming from the cool roof chamber? How did this help Ehud escape? How is this part of the story ironic?_____

   _____

   _____

   _____

   _____

   e. What trickery did Ehud use to gain private access to King Eglon? Why do you think this trickery was successful?_____

   _____

   _____

   _____

   _____

Challenge Yourself!

Read the Gospel of John 9:1-12.

1. What does the Gospel of John 9:1-3 tell us about the culture of ancient Israel (in fact the culture throughout the ancient Near East) as to the thinking of people regarding the cause of illness and disease? Relate your answer to ancient religious beliefs._____

   _____
   _____
   _____
   _____
   _____
   _____
   _____
   _____
   _____
   _____
   _____
   _____
   _____
   _____
   _____

2. Continue reading this account through John 9:12. How did Yeshua refute this idea and elevate the people's understanding about the God of Israel? (Hint: carefully consider Yeshua's words, "Go wash in the Pool of Siloam," and practice asking yourself questions).____

   _____
   _____
   _____
   _____
   _____
   _____
   _____
   _____
   _____
   _____
   _____
   _____
   _____

Application Questions

1. Consider the verses you have read – Judges 3:9, 15; 4:3; 6:6-7; 10:10. What would be a teaching outline for the message that these verses convey? Start by introducing the message. Then include the historical background of the Period of the Judges and explain how the same situation exists in our lives today. Finally, give at least one example from the Book of Judges that demonstrates the message._____

\
\
\
\
\
\
\
\
\
\
\
\
\
\
\
\
\

2. You have been learning to ask questions that stimulate curiosity and help penetrate a deeper understanding of the biblical text. Read Judges 11:1-11 about Jephthah. What are 10 questions you might ask about this passage that could start you on a journey to uncover its depth of meaning?_____

\
\
\
\
\
\
\
\
\
\
\
\
\
\
\
\
\

Chapter 2 Quiz

1. Where were the Israelites living during the Period of the Judges?
   a. The coastal plain
   b. The hill country
   c. The northern kingdom of Israel
   d. The southern kingdom of Judah

2. Following are some of the tribes that were allocated land in the Promised Land: Asher, Zebulun, Issachar, Ephraim, Gad, Dan, Benjamin, and Simeon. What four tribes are missing from this list? _____
   _____
   _____

3. What followed the Period of the Judges?
   a. Exodus from Egypt
   b. Divided Kingdom
   c. United Kingdom
   d. Babylonian Captivity

4. In the account of the woman who had a hemorrhage for twelve years, she approached Yeshua by:
   a. walking behind him timidly and slowly because that was the cultural practice of women
   b. boldly walking through the crowd with faith in order to reach him
   c. pushing the men aside as she moved from the edge of the crowd to reach the master
   d. crawling on her hands and knees so no one would see her

5. In the divided kingdom, the northern kingdom was called _____ with its capital at _____, and the southern kingdom was called _____ with its capital at _____?

6. The ten northern tribes were taken into captivity by:
   a. Babylon
   b. Persia
   c. Assyria
   d. Rome

7. Hezekiah was:
   a. Prophet of Israel
   b. Prophet of Judah
   c. King of Israel
   d. King of Judah

8. What does Ehud's being left-handed tell us about the culture of Israel?
   a. Handicapped people were considered cursed
   b. Swords were typically sheathed on the right hip
   c. A left-handed man was more likely to be admitted into the presence of a king than a right-handed man
   d. Being left-handed made Ehud a better warrior

9. The name Siloam has meaning which signifies:
   a. Washing away sins
   b. Miraculous healing
   c. Disciples who were sent to minister to God's people
   d. Those who believed that Yeshua was the promised Messiah

10. Eglon was kind of the
   e. Moabites
   f. Ammonites
   g. Hittites
   h. Amelekites

Chapter 3
Mysterious Artistry of Biblical Poetry

Summary

This is a very important chapter because it introduces you to the artistic nature of the biblical language. The best way to learn and practice is through poetic passages. We all hear the rhythm and feel the emotion of the psalms, which are all poetic. However, this chapter will show you how to uncover a depth of meaning by listening to the relationships between the poetic parallel lines.

Outline of Lecture

BIBLICAL POETRY

I.   Characteristics

    A. Rhythm, not rhyme

    B. Listen – rhythm evokes emotion

    C. Organize the parallel lines

    D. Relationship between parallel lines stimulates meaning

II.   Psalm 32:1-5

> [1]*How blessed is he*
>   *Whose transgression is forgiven,*
>   *Whose sin is covered!*
> [2]*How blessed is the man*
>   *to whom the LORD does not impute iniquity,*
>   *And in whose spirit there is no deceit!*

    A. Repetition

    B. Organize artistic structure

> [1]*How blessed is he*
>   *Whose <u>transgression</u> is <u>forgiven</u>,*

    C. Whose <u>sin</u> is <u>covered</u>.

    D. Verses 1-2

A Blessing
1. Transgression is <u>forgiven</u>
2. Sin is <u>covered</u>

1. Forgives sin – covers

   a. Echo – God covered the sins of Adam and Eve

   b. Covered with skins of an animal (unblemished sacrifice to God)

2. Relationship: Cause and Effect (forgiveness)

Main Character	Action
The Lord	Does not impute iniquity
Person with an inner spirit	Has no deceit

E. Verses 3-4

³ When I kept silent about my sin,
my body wasted away
through my groaning all day long.
⁴ For day and night Your hand was heavy upon me;
my vitality was drained away
as with the fever heat of summer.

1. Parallel lines

2. Relationships

F. Verse 5

FIRST PARALLEL LINES   *⁵ I acknowledged my sin to You,*
and my iniquity I did not hide; I said,

SECOND PARALLEL LINES *"I will confess my transgressions to the LORD";*
And You forgave the guilt of my sin.

1. Parallel lines

2. Relationships

III.   Review artistic relationship of parallel lines

IV.   Isaiah 11:1-2

A. Verse 1

¹ A shoot will spring
from the stem of Jesse,
And a branch
from his roots will bear fruit

1. Rhythm and emotion

2. Parallel relationship

   a. Metaphor

   b. Imagery and symbolism of spiritual growth

      1) New life (seed)

      2) Mature

      3) Bear fruit

B. Verse 2

   ² The Spirit of the LORD will rest on Him,
   The spirit of wisdom and understanding,
   The spirit of counsel and strength,
   The spirit of knowledge and the fear of the LORD

   1. Rhythm

   2. Parallel relationships

The Spirit of the Lord is:	
Wisdom (skilled and wise)	Understanding (discern good & evil)
Counsel (Guide)	Strength (Power)
Knowledge (know the truth)	Fear of the Lord (come into His presence)

   3. The Spirit of the Lord is…

      a. Wisdom

      b. Understanding

      c. Counsel

      d. Strength

      e. Knowledge – Pr 15:14

      f. Fear of the Lord – 2 Chr 19:17; Ps 111:10

Words to be Defined

1. Biblical Poetry _____

   _____

   _____

2. Parallel Lines _____

   _____

   _____

Questions for Comprehension

1. What is the difference between biblical poetry and western poetry that rhymes?_____

   _____

   _____

   _____

   _____

   _____

2. How do the parallel lines in Psalm 32:2 convey cause and effect?_____

   _____

   _____

   _____

   _____

   _____

3. In Isaiah 11:1, who is the shoot that will spring from the root of Jesse? Explain your answer._____

   _____

   _____

   _____

   _____

   _____

4. Who are the branches that are bearing fruit? Explain your answer._____

   _____

   _____

   _____

   _____

   _____

5. Isaiah 11:2 lists six attributes that come to mankind from the Spirit of the Lord. List and explain each one.

_____

_____

_____

_____

_____

_____

Building Skills

1. Now it is time for you to practice perceiving the artistic nature of Hebrew poetry and exploring the meaning that results.

    a. Read Psalm 1 aloud. Listen to the rhythm and feel the emotion.

    b. What repetition do you hear? _____

    _____

    _____

    c. What contrast do you hear? _____

    _____

    _____

    _____

    d. In the space below, write verse 1 in a way that displays its artistic form.

    e. What is the relationship between the three lines in verse 1? _____

    _____

    _____

    _____

f. What is the relationship between the two parallel lines in verse 2?_____

_____

_____

_____

_____

g. What is the relationship between verses 2 and 3?_____

_____

_____

_____

_____

h. From this exercise, write in your own words the meaning that results from the artistry of this psalm__

_____

_____

_____

_____

2. You will continue working in Psalm 1, but this time you will focus on "contrast." The English word "but" indicates a contrast.

a. "But" appears three times in Psalm 1. Identify and write below the three contrasts followed by your thoughts regarding the meaning of each._____

_____

_____

_____

_____

_____

b. Although there is no word "but," how are verses 1-3 a contrast to verses 4-6?_____

_____

_____

_____

_____

c. How does Psalm 1 define a wicked person?_____

_____

_____

_____

_____

d. Psalm 1 identifies one way that a person can be blessed in verse 1, and another way in verse 2. Describe these two positive actions._____

_____

_____

_____

_____

_____

_____

Challenge Yourself!

You are now ready to dig even deeper into the meaning of Psalm 1.

1. Imagery is a powerful linguistic tool. Verses 4-5 use the imagery of winnowing grain to portray God's future judgment. Describe the agricultural practice of winnowing, and explain how this imagery is used to portray judgment._____

_____

_____

_____

_____

2. How does the agricultural practice of winnowing apply to Isaiah 41:14-16? What is the message that this imagery in Isaiah conveys?_____

_____

_____

_____

_____

3. Returning to Psalm 1, we must reflect on an important Hebrew concept that uses the words הלך (halak, walk) and דרך (derek, way or path) to convey the direction in our lives and the choices we make. These two words are both used in the first verse 1, and דרך is used twice in the last verse 6. Thus, there is a parallel relationship between these two verses (1 and 6). Furthermore, the verses between them give us advice on how to walk in God's ways. Explain this advice in your own words below._____

_____

_____

_____

_____

_____

Questions for Discussion

1. Carefully read Psalm 32 again.

   a. What is the relationship between God's forgiveness and His covering our sins?_____

   _____

   _____

   _____

   b. How is covering our sins an echo of the story of Adam and Eve, and what does that story in Genesis teach us about the relationship between God's covering our sins and the symbolic meaning of sacrifice?_____

   _____

   _____

   _____

   c. How do we transport this symbolism into our lives today?_____

   _____

   _____

   _____

2. Read Robert Frost's poem, "Stopping by Woods on a Snowy Evening." You will find both similarities and differences between this poem and Psalm 32.

   a. What are the similarities?_____

   _____

   _____

   _____

   _____

   _____

   _____

   b. What are the differences?_____

   _____

   _____

   _____

   _____

   _____

   _____

   _____

Stopping by Woods on a Snowy Evening
By Robert Frost

Whose woods these are I think I know.
His house is in the village though;
He will not see me stopping here
To watch his woods fill up with snow.

My little horse must think it queer
To stop without a farmhouse near
Between the woods and frozen lake
The darkest evening of the year.

He gives his harness bells a shake
To ask if there is some mistake.
The only other sound's the sweep
Of easy wind and downy flake.

The woods are lovely, dark and deep,
But I have promises to keep,
And miles to go before I sleep,
And miles to go before I sleep.

Read Psalm 22.

1. This psalm is divided into two parts. What verses constitute the first part, and what verses constitute the second part?_____

_____

_____

_____

_____

_____

2. What is the contrast between the two parts?_____

_____

_____

_____

_____

3. What is the imagery and symbolism in the first part, and what meaning does this imagery and symbolism convey?_____

_____

_____

_____

_____

4. How does the first part apply to your life?_____

_____

_____

_____

_____

5. What is the message of the second part?_____

_____

_____

_____

_____

6. What specific words, imagery and symbolism convey this message?_____

_____

_____

_____

_____

Application Questions

1. The message conveyed by the poetic artistry of Psalm 32 gave us much to think about. We learned that God's forgiveness only covers our sins. Then we learned there is more to God's forgiveness. In our daily walk with God, we must strive to become the unblemished sacrificial animal in order for the forgiveness of sins to become complete.

   a. Is this a new concept for you regarding forgiveness of sins? What is your traditional understanding?

   _____

   _____

   _____

   _____

   _____

   _____

   _____

   _____

   _____

   b. How does Yeshua cover our sins?_____

   _____

   _____

   _____

   c. How might you strive to become (metaphorically) an unblemished animal that God will accept?_____

   _____

   _____

   _____

   _____

   d. God has already accepted you into His family when you first believed in His son. But then He encourages you to walk in a righteous path SO THAT you can draw near to Him. How have you experienced drawing near to God in your life?_____

   _____

   _____

   _____

   _____

   _____

   _____

2. Read Isaiah 11:1-2 again.

    a. Where are you in your stage of spiritual growth? Are you still a seed?_____

_____

_____

_____

_____

_____

_____

_____

_____

_____

_____

_____

    b. Are you in the process of maturing, and if so, where are you in that process?_____

_____

_____

_____

_____

_____

_____

_____

_____

_____

_____

_____

    c. Are you bearing fruit for God? If so, give an example._____

_____

_____

_____

_____

_____

_____

_____

_____

_____

_____

_____

Chapter 3 Quiz

1. The most important key to understanding the meaning embedded in parallel lines is:

    a. rhythm that leads to emotion
    b. repetition and contrast
    c. relationship between the lines
    d. key words

2. Repetition in Hebrew poetry is always synonymous.

    a. True
    b. False

3. The main message in Psalm 32 is:

    a. Mankind sins
    b. God forgives
    c. Repentance leads to forgiveness
    d. Sins lead to consequences

4. Contrast is often conveyed by the English word:

    a. but
    b. and
    c. so
    d. neither/nor

5. Match the following words (in English translation), which appear in Isaiah 11:1-2, with their meaning.

    _____Wisdom   A. Know the truth

    _____Understanding   B. Skilled and wise

    _____Counsel   C. Discern good and evil

    _____Strength   D. Guide

    _____Knowledge   E. Power

6. What is chaff?

    a. Seed
    b. Fruit
    c. Kernel
    d. Bran

7. To best display the artistic nature of Hebrew poetry, one can use:

    a. Indenting
    b. Capital letters
    c. Italics
    d. Parenthesis

8. The nature of Hebrew poetry will always convey a sense of emotion through rhythm.

    a. True
    b. False

9. The purpose of a threshing sledge is to:
    a. Separate good from evil
    b. Separate weeds from good plants
    c. Separate sins from transgressions
    d. Separate seed from chaff

10. Psalm 32 creates a relationship between:
    a. Blessing and cursing
    b. Truth and deceit
    c. Forgiveness and covering
    d. Contrast and synonyms

Chapter 4
Key Words

Summary

Now that you know the Hebrew alphabet, it is time for you to begin identifying key words, which you will see first in English. However, you will then be able to identify the original Hebrew word. Once you know the Hebrew word you can use the online interlinear Bible to gain an understanding of the meaning of the Hebrew word, not the English translation.

Outline of Lecture

I.   Tools

      A.   Lexicon

      B.   Concordance – www.biblos.com

II.   Practice with Genesis 3:8

      A.   Six steps

           1.   Start with a particular word in a specific verse – e.g. "cool of the day" (Gen 3:8)

           2.   Click on Interlinear

3. Enter your verse

4. Find your word and click on Strong's number

5. Strong's definition is on the top left (number of occurrences at the top right)

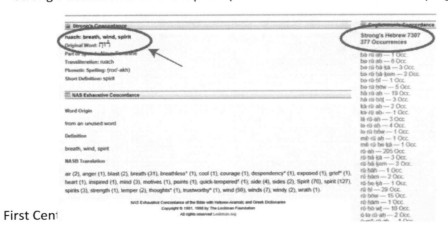

First Cent

6. In the right column you will find a list of all the verses in which your word appears

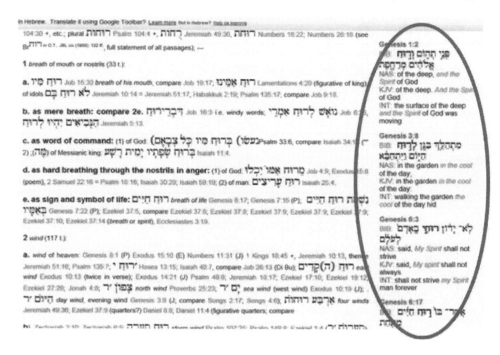

B. Uncovering the meaning of the word.

1. Make a list of all the verses in which the word appears

2. Take BRIEF notes on the meaning of the word (how it is used) in each verse

3. From your notes, you will be able to see various nuances of meaning

    a. Always consider the first usage of the word first

    b. Then examine how the word is used in subsequent verses

4. From your notes, you will be able to see a pattern of how the word is used

III.   Practice with Genesis 4:2-5

A. Finding a key word

1. Be curious

2. Ask yourself questions

B. Verse 2 - contrast

Abel was a keeper of flocks,

BUT Cain was a tiller of the ground.

C. Verses 3-4

> ³So it came about in the course of time that
> > Cain brought an offering to the Lord of the fruit of the ground.
> > > ⁴Abel, on his part, also brought of the firstling of his flock
> > > > and of their fat portions.

1. Contrast

2. Something added – "and of their fat portions"

D. Verse 5 – startled by a repetition

> The LORD had regard for Abel and for his offering;
> ⁵but for Cain and for his offering He had no regard.

1. Repetition – "regard"

2. Hebrew word - שעה (shaah) = to gaze intently

3. Picture in your mind

E. Verse 4 – startled because something has been added.

> It came about in the course of time that
> Cain brought an offering to the Lord of the fruit of the ground.
> Abel, on his part, also brought of the of the <u>firstlings</u> of his flock
> > and of their fat portions.

1. Firstlings –

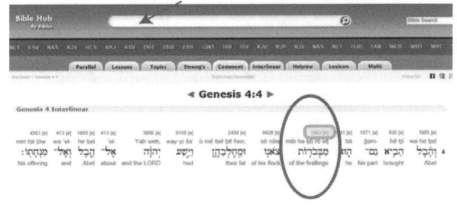

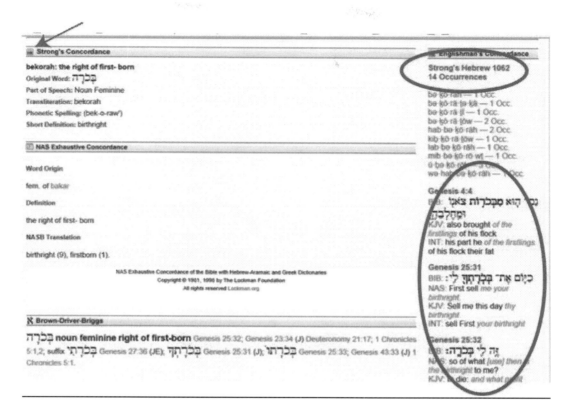

a. Conduct a word study

b. Sometimes used for people – Ex 4:22

c. Sometimes used for animals

d. Abel gave the firstborn animal AND their fat portions (burned as a sweet incense to God during the sacrifice of the firstborn animal)

Words to be Defined

1. Lexicon _____

   _____

   _____

2. Concordance _____

   _____

   _____

3. Interlinear Bible _____

   _____

   _____

Questions for Comprehension

1. Why does Dr. Davis encourage you to use the Interlinear Bible in www.biblos.com instead of Strong's Concordance? _____

   _____

   _____

2. What are the six steps for conducting a word study?_____

   _____

   _____

   _____

3. After completing the six steps, what is the purpose of making a list of verses where the Hebrew word appears in Scripture?_____

   _____

   _____

   _____

4. Where does רוח first appear in Scripture? How is the Hebrew word used there? _____

   _____

   _____

   _____

5. How do you identify a key word in Scripture?_____

   _____

   _____

   _____

6. What drew our attention to שעה in Genesis 4:4-5?_____

   _____

   _____

   _____

7. Dr. Davis was drawn to the word "firstling" in Genesis 4:4. What did she do after she became curious about the meaning of this word?_____

   _____

   _____

   _____

Building Skills

1. It is important that you practice using www.biblos.com to understand the meaning of a word with its Hebraic nuance of meaning instead of relying on the English translation. We have already used

www.biblos.com to identify "cool" (NASB) in Gen 3:8. Go now to www.biblos.com to find Gen 3:8. Click on the number for Strong's definition of "cool," and then locate the list of verses that contain this Hebrew word. We have listed the first two verses for you, but you should scroll down to see all of them.

Genesis 1:2

HEB: פְנֵי תְהֹום **וְרוּחַ** אֱלֹהִים מְרַחֶפֶת

NAS: of the deep, and the Spirit of God

KJV: of the deep. And the Spirit of God

INT: the surface of the deep and the Spirit of God was moving

Genesis 3:8

HEB: מִתְהַלֵּךְ בַּגָּן **לְרוּחַ** הַיֹּום וַיִּתְחַבֵּא

NAS: in the garden in the cool of the day,

KJV: in the garden in the cool of the day:

INT: walking the garden the cool of the day hid

a. What is the Hebrew word?_____

b. How many total verses contain this Hebrew word?_____

c. We have already discussed the first two usages in Gen 1:2 and Gen 3:8. Now, in the space provided, write out in English the next 5 verses that contain this Hebrew word and circle the English word that has been used to translate it.

d. How does "breath" and "wind" help you understand the nature of God?_____

_____

_____

_____

_____

e. How do these 5 verses help you understand Gen 3:8?_____

_____

_____

_____

_____

2. Read Gen 4:2-5.

a. Let yourself be curious. What questions does your curiosity stimulate from these 4 verses?_____

_____

_____

b. Why is "offering" a key word in this passage?_____

_____

_____

c. Use www.biblos.com to look up the Hebrew word that has been translated "offering" (NASB). How many times is this Hebrew word used in the Torah?_____

d. The Hebrew word is used 4 times in Gen 32 and 4 times again in Gen 43. Carefully read these two passages in Genesis. Then, from the context of what you have read, explain the nuance of the meaning of this Hebrew word._____

_____

_____

_____

Questions for Discussion

1. What was the interpretation of Dr. Davis as to why God chose Abel instead of Cain? What was her evidence for this interpretation? Do you agree or disagree? Explain your answer. _____

_____

_____

_____

_____

_____

_____

_____

Challenge Yourself!

In the lecture, Dr. Davis took you to Genesis 4:4 where we read, *"Abel brought of the firstling of his flock."* You saw that the Hebrew word that has been translated "firstling" (NASB) is בְּכֹרָה. Strong's Concordance gives us the definition, *"the right of the firstborn."* However, I have urged you not to rely on Strong's English definition of an English word. So, the challenge before you now is to conduct a word study of the verses where בְּכֹרָה appear. Use www.biblos.com to answer the following questions.

1. How many times does בְּכֹרָה . appear in Scripture?_____

2. What is the first appearance of בְּכֹרָה.?_____

3. How many times does בְּכֹרָה. refer to the firstborn son who was entitled to the inheritance of the birthright?_____

4. How many times does בְּכֹרָה. refer to a firstborn animal?_____

5. What is the relationship between a firstborn son and a firstborn animal?_____
_____
_____
_____
_____

Application Questions

1. How can we take the symbolism of God's accepting Abel's sacrifice and apply it to our lives today?_____
_____
_____
_____
_____
_____
_____
_____
_____
_____
_____
_____
_____
_____

2. Have you ever thought that some interpretations of the Bible may not be exactly correct? If you wanted to search the Scriptures for your own conclusions, you could start with one word and then conduct a word study.

   a. What are some questions that you might be asking about biblical interpretations?_____

   _____
   _____
   _____
   _____
   _____
   _____
   _____
   _____
   _____
   _____
   _____
   _____
   _____
   _____
   _____

   b. How would you go about doing a word study to try and find a biblical answer to your questions?____

   _____
   _____
   _____
   _____
   _____
   _____
   _____
   _____
   _____
   _____
   _____
   _____
   _____
   _____

Chapter 4 Quiz

1. What is the primary function of a dictionary?
    a. list all the verses in which a word is located
    b. alphabetize a list of words
    c. give a definition for each word
    d. explain how a word is pronounced

2. What is the primary function of a lexicon?
    a. list all the verses in which a word is located
    b. alphabetize a list of words
    c. give a definition for each word
    d. explain how a word is pronounced

3. What is the primary function of a concordance?
    a. list all the verses in which a word is located
    b. alphabetize a list of words
    c. give a definition for each word
    d. explain how a word is pronounced

4. Why does Dr. Davis caution you against relying on Strong's Concordance?
    a. The publication is out of date
    b. There is no listing of the original Hebrew or Greek word
    c. There is no list of verses in which the word appears
    d. Definitions are given in English

5. The Hebrew word רוּחַ has been translated in various ways including:
    a. God, Spirit and wind
    b. God, Spirit and breath
    c. God, wind and breath
    d. Spirit, wind and breath

6. The Hebrew word רוּחַ first appears in:
    a. Gen 1:1
    b. Gen 1:2
    c. Gen 1:4
    d. Gen 3:8

7. Abel brought the "firstlings" of his flock, which is a translation of the Hebrew word that means:
    a. pure
    b. unblemished
    c. firstborn
    d. righteous

8. "Firstlings of his flock and of their fat portions" refers to:

    a. A burnt offering on the altar

    b. Burning of incense on the altar

    c. Service only by the high priest

    d. Service by all the priests

9. A key word can often be identified by:

    a. repetition

    b. contrast

    c. something strange or unusual

    d. all of the above

10. Why did God refuse Cain's offering?

    a. It was blemished

    b. It was not the best Cain had to offer

    c. It was not a burnt offering

    d. All of the above

Chapter 5
Imagery and Symbolism

Summary

You have been working with the artistic nature of the biblical language. In this chapter, you will continue to practice listening to the text for anything that is startling, that is, for anything that the ancient ear would have heard as something unusual. You will now be working with images that evoke a picture in your mind, symbols where one thing means another, and metaphors that are extended symbols. Metaphors may be hard to recognize at first, but they are prevalent throughout Scripture so we will spend time working with metaphors.

Outline of Lecture

I.   Introduction – searching the Scriptures, not Bible study

II.   Imagery

    A. David – 1 Sam 16:12

III.   Imagery and symbolism combined – The story of Deborah

    A. Geography

        1. Deborah from the hill country of Ephraim

        2. Deborah called Barak from Naphtali to command Israel's army

        3. Battle took place in the Jezreel Valley

    B. Deborah was the only woman judge

        1. Barak's response – Judges 4:8

        2. The battle

    C. Jael, the heroine – Judges 5:24

        1. Sisera, the enemy commander, flees on foot to Jael's tent

        2. Seductress

        3. Mother

        4. Warrior

        5. Victor

    D. Irony in the story

IV.   Symbol – one thing represents another

    A. Wine is blood of Christ

    B. Bread is body of Christ

    C. Tent peg and hammer represent tools of women

    D. What does Jael represent?

V. Problem – how does Scripture convey the nature of God and spiritual matters?

    1. God is Spirit - Represented by wind and breath

    2. Need a metaphor

VI. Metaphor

    A. Extended symbol

    B. A symbol with no literal relationship

    C. "A might fortress is our God"

    D. Another example

> *My people have committed two evils:*
>
>   1. *They have forsaken Me,*
>   *The fountain of living waters,*
>   2. *To hew for themselves cisterns,*
>   *Broken cisterns that can hold no water.* Jer 2:13

Words to be Defined

1. Kennites_____

_____

_____

2. Imagery_____

_____

_____

3. Symbol_____

_____

_____

4. Metaphor_____

_____

_____

Questions for Comprehension

1. Describe the imagery of the story of Deborah the judge from her call to Barak to the victory of the battle in the Jezreel Valley. _____

_____

_____

_____

_____

_____

2. Who was Jael?_____

_____

3. What are the symbols in the story of Jael, and what do the symbols represent?_____

_____

_____

_____

4. How was Jael a seductress? A mother? A warrior? A victor? _____

_____

_____

_____

5. What is the difference between a symbol and a metaphor?_____

_____

_____

_____

6. How is "A mighty fortress is our God" a metaphor?_____

_____

_____

_____

7. How is calling God "a fountain of living waters" a metaphor?_____

_____

_____

_____

Building Skills

1. Your Bible atlas should be a tool that you use constantly. In this exercise, you will use your Bible atlas to learn more about the Period of the Judges.

   a. Identify when the period of the Judges occurred.

   b. Find where the 12 tribes settled in the land of Canaan.

   c. Locate the tribal area where Deborah came from, the tribal area where Barak came from, and Hazor, the walled city where the enemy was located. Why do you think the battle was fought in the Jezreel Valley?_____

_____

_____

_____

_____

d. Learn more in your Bible atlas about the Kennites. Take brief notes here._____

_____

_____

_____

_____

_____

_____

_____

_____

2. Now read the Book of Judges in your Bible. Read it as a story but listen for the artistic nature of the biblical language. There will be questions in the quiz at the end of this chapter on the Period of the Judges.

Questions for Discussion

1. There are three metaphors in 2 Samuel 22:3

    a. What are the three metaphors? _____

    _____

    _____

    b. Try your best to give a brief literal description of taking refuge in a rock (perceiving it as a literal symbol will be very difficult)._____

    _____

    _____

    _____

    c. Discuss how the symbols are extended to become metaphors that have no literal meaning._____

    _____

    _____

    _____

    _____

    d. What is the extended meaning of each metaphor?_____

    _____

    _____

    _____

    _____

2. Now consider the metaphor in Isaiah 66:1, *"Heaven is My throne."*

    a. To understand this metaphor you must first see it as a symbol. Therefore, Isaiah sees one word which is _____ to represent another word which is _____

b. Do your best to briefly describe a physical image of heaven as a throne (perceiving it as a literal symbol will be very difficult). _____

_____

_____

_____

_____

_____

_____

_____

_____

c. *"Heaven is My throne"* is more than a simple symbol. It has become a metaphor, which goes beyond the literal image. Explain the deeper meaning of the metaphor, *"Heaven is My throne."* _____

_____

_____

_____

_____

_____

_____

_____

3. What is irony and what makes it ironic? How is the story of Deborah conveyed with irony? What is the purpose of the irony? _____

_____

_____

_____

_____

_____

_____

_____

4. How does wind and breath metaphorically convey God as Spirit? _____

_____

_____

_____

_____

_____

_____

Challenge Yourself!

Compare Judges chapters 4 and 5 about the story of Deborah.

1. How is chapter 4 a narrative?_____

2. How is chapter 5 a victory song by the women?_____

3. What are the similarities between the two chapters? How are they different?_____
   _____
   _____
   _____
   _____
   _____
   _____
   _____
   _____
   _____
   _____
   _____
   _____

4. Why do scholars suggest that Chapter 4 was written after the Period of the Judges ended, possibly during the reign of King David?_____
   _____
   _____
   _____
   _____
   _____
   _____
   _____
   _____
   _____
   _____
   _____
   _____

Application Questions

1. Do you ever use irony? What are some examples? When is the use of irony appropriate in our culture and when is it not?_____

_____

_____

_____

_____

_____

_____

_____

_____

_____

_____

_____

_____

_____

_____

_____

2. What message do you think the story of Deborah and Barak is conveying to women in the United States today? If women see that men are not fulfilling their expected roles, what should they do?._____

_____

_____

_____

_____

_____

_____

_____

_____

_____

_____

_____

_____

_____

_____

_____

Chapter 5 Quiz

1. How many judges were there?

   a. Six
   b. Seven
   c. Ten
   d. Twelve

2. Who was the first judge?

   a. Barak
   b. Othniel
   c. Samson
   d. Gideon

3. Who was the last judge?

   a. Barak
   b. Othniel
   c. Samson
   d. Gideon

4. Who was the left-handed judge who killed the kind of Moab?

   a. Jephthah
   b. Shamgar
   c. Ehud
   d. Tola

5. Who was the only woman judge?_____

6. What was the most common period of time of rest between the judges?

   a. Ten years
   b. Twenty years
   c. Thirty years
   d. Forty years

7. When did God raise up a judge??

   a. When the people repented
   b. When the people cried out to the Lord
   c. When the enemy came into the settlements of the Israelites
   d. When the people prayed to God

8. Which judge was blinded by the Philistines?

   a. Gideon
   b. Shamgar
   c. Samson
   d. Jephthah

9. Which judge was the son of a harlot?
    a. Gideon
    b. Shamgar
    c. Samson
    d. Jephthah

10. Who was the judge at the time that the Israelites defeated Sisera, the commander of the troops for the kind of Hazor?
    a. Deborah
    b. Othniel
    c. Barak
    d. Gideon

Chapter 6
Names and Numbers

Summary

This chapter will begin by briefly reviewing how Christianity lost its connection to the Hebraic approach to viewing Scripture and created instead a Greek model for studying the Bible. Then we will see that every time a name or number appears in Scripture, one must stop to consider the possibility of symbolism. We will end by exploring the deeper meaning of the name of Abram that God changed to Abraham, and then we will look at the symbolism of the number forty.

Outline of Lecture

I.   Introduction to the course

    A.   Listen to the text

    B.   Six linquistic devices

II. What happened that caused us to shift from thinking Hebrew to thinking Greek?

    A.   First century (time of Yeshua)

    B.   Four events that contributed to the shift

III. Abraham's name

    A.   Avram – Gen 12:1-2

    B.   Avram's name changed to Abraham

        1.   Gen 17:1-2

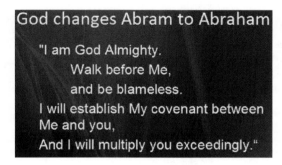

        2.   "I will multiply you exceedingly"

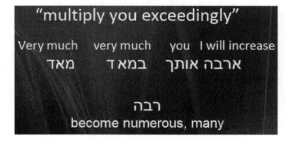

3. Chiasm of Gen 17:4-5

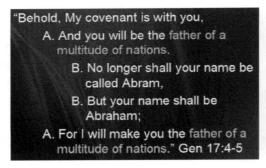

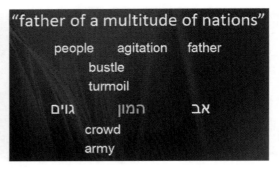

C. Abraham's blessing expanded

1. Gen 22:17

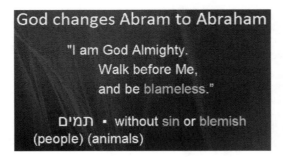

D. Abraham a righteous remnant

1. Gen 18:19

> I have chosen him, so that he may
> command his children and his household
> after him to keep the way of the LORD by
> > doing righteousness
> > and justice,
> so that the LORD may bring upon
> Abraham what He has spoken about him.
> Gen 18:19
>
> ### Righteous Remnant

2. "Walk before me and be blameless"

3. Word study on "blameless" – Gen 6:9; 7:23

> ## God changes Abram to Abraham
>
> "I am God Almighty.
> Walk before Me,
> and be blameless."
>
> תמים · without sin or blemish
> (people) (animals)

IV. The number forty
   A. Repeated cycle in the Book of Judges

   B. The number 40 in Judges

   C. E. W. Bullinger, *Numbers in Scripture* (www.levendwater.org)

   D. Period of probation, trial & chastisement

      1. 40 years

      2. 40 days

      3. Book of Judges – all are 40 years of rest EXCEPT Judges 13:1

Words to be Defined

1. Tanakh_____
_____
_____

2. Torah_____
_____
_____

3. Nevi'im_____
_____
_____

4. Ketuvim_____
_____
_____

5. Dispersion_____
_____
_____

6. *Sola scriptura*_____
_____
_____

7. *Sola literalis*_____
_____
_____

Questions for Comprehension

1. What is the Tanakh? How and why is the Tanakh different from the Christian Bible today? _____

    _____

    _____

2. When was the destruction of the temple by the Romans, and how did that lead to a dispersion of the Jews?_____

    _____

    _____

    _____

3. Who was Bar Kochba?_____

    _____

4. Who was the Roman emperor at the time of the Council of Nicaea in 323 A.D.? What two decisions were made there that helped shape the kind of Bible study that is in common use today? _____

    _____

    _____

    _____

5. What was Abraham's name before it was changed, and what did his first name mean?_____

    _____

    _____

6. What does the name Abraham mean? Explain how this new name is prophetic._____

    _____

    _____

    _____

7. According to E. W. Bullinger, what does the number 40 represent in Scripture? Give five examples of this symbolic number in Scripture._____

    _____

    _____

    _____

    _____

Building Skills

1. Chiasm is an ancient literary device that uses parallel lines to point to a chiastic center. There will always be a relationship between the parallel lines, and the relationship will convey a sense of meaning. Consider the parallel lines below (A lines and B lines).

A. *You will be the father of a multitude of nations.*

    B. *No longer shall your name be called Abram,*

    B. *But your name shall be Abraham;*

A. *For I will make you the father of a multitude of nations* (Gen 17:4-5)

a.   What is the relationship between the A lines?_____

_____

_____

_____

_____

b.   What is the relationship between the B lines?_____

_____

_____

_____

_____

c.   What is the relationship between the A lines and the chiastic center (B lines)?_____

_____

_____

_____

_____

2.   The Hebrew word תמים appears in Genesis 17:1.

a.   What does תמים mean?_____

_____

b.   Each of the following verses contains the word תמים. Read each verse **in its context** (include the surrounding verses that give it a full meaning). Take brief notes on the meaning of תמים in each verse.

Genesis 6:9_____

_____

_____

Genesis 17:1_____

_____

_____

Exodus 12:5_____

_____

_____

Deuteronomy 18:13_____

_____

_____

_____

Deuteronomy 32:4_____

_____

_____

_____

3. Each of the following verses contains the word תמים. Read each verse in its context (include the surrounding verses that give it a full meaning). Take brief notes on the meaning of תמים in each verse.

Matthew 5:48_____

_____

_____

_____

_____

Romans_____

_____

_____

_____

_____

Hebrews 6:1_____

_____

_____

_____

_____

4. In your own words, give a full and complete description of.תמים (translated τέλειος in the New Testament)._____

_____

_____

_____

_____

_____

_____

_____

_____

_____

Challenge Yourself!

You will now be working on the spiritual meaning of the number six.

1. With one sentence write what Bullinger gives as the spiritual meaning of the number six.____
   _____
   _____

2. The first usage of the number six appears in Gen 1:31. Where does the context of this particular verse begin?_____
   _____
   _____
   _____

3. What is the sixth clause of the Lord's Prayer, and how does the symbolism of the number six relate to this clause in the Lord's Prayer?_____
   _____
   _____
   _____

4. How do the first six days of creation in Genesis relate to Exodus 20:9 and Deuteronomy 5:13? (Do not address the 7th day of creation, only the first 6 days)._____
   _____
   _____
   _____
   _____
   _____
   _____
   _____

Questions for Discussion

1. Consider the following chiastic structure.
   A. *I have chosen him, so that he may command his children and his household after him to keep the way of the LORD by*
      B. *doing righteousness*
      B. *and justice,*
   A. *so that the LORD may bring upon Abraham what He has spoken about him.* (Gen 18:19)

a. What makes these lines chiastic? _____

_____

_____

b. In the first A line you can hear "so that," which indicates a consequence. What is the action that causes a consequence, and what is the consequence._____

_____

_____

_____

_____

c. What is the relationship between the two A lines?_____

_____

_____

_____

_____

2. God is urging us, in the same words He spoke to Abraham, to "walk before Him and be perfect." What do you think it means to "walk before God?"_____

_____

_____

_____

_____

_____

3. Have you been taught to simply "read the literal words of Scripture?" What impact do you think this tradition has had on Christianity??_____

_____

_____

_____

_____

_____

4. Before taking this course, how did you interpret the deeper meaning of Scripture? Has this course changed the way you now interpret the Scriptures?_____

_____

_____

_____

_____

_____

Ponder how the meaning of Noah's name relates to the creation in Genesis 1-2 to the end of time when God's work will be complete, and to what God is doing in the world today._____

_____

_____

_____

_____

_____

_____

_____

There are six lamps in the menorah, three on either side of the central lamp, which equals a total of seven lamps. Therefore, the menorah contains four numbers, all of which have spiritual significance – 1, 3, 6, 7. How do these numbers convey a spiritual meaning in the menorah?_____

_____

_____

_____

_____

_____

_____

_____

_____

In the lecture, Dr. Davis discussed the change of Abram's name to Abraham. Follow this same pattern and discuss the change of Sarai's name to Sarah, and Jacob's name to Israel._____

_____

_____

_____

_____

_____

_____

_____

_____

Application Questions

1. Only Yeshua the Messiah was without sin and therefore תמים. Yet God asks us to be תמים. It may not be possible to be.תמים at all times in our lives, but we can stretch and reach for this goal. Think of five things you can do in your life to help you "walk before God and be תמים." How do you plan to achieve these goals?_____

   _____

   _____

   _____

   _____

   _____

   _____

   _____

   _____

   _____

   _____

   _____

   _____

2. The biblical narrative is more than a story because it is designed to teach us about God and our relationship with Him. Consider the forty years of wilderness wandering after the Exodus. What do these forty years represent? Give at least three specific examples from the wilderness account. How can the wilderness wandering be applied to your own life?_____

   _____

   _____

   _____

   _____

   _____

   _____

   _____

   _____

   _____

   _____

   _____

   _____

Chapter 6 Quiz

1. Who were the first Christians?

   a. Jews
   b. Sadducees
   c. Essenes
   d. Those who believed that Yeshua was the prophet whom God had prophesied to Moses

2. The first Christians did not have access to the New Testament.

   a. True
   b. False

3. When was the temple destroyed by the Romans?

   a. 30 BC
   b. 30 AD
   c. 70 AD
   d. 135 AD

4. What were the two significant decisions made at the time of the Council of Nicaea?

   a. Separated the two testaments and gave it priority by placing it first.
   b. Separated the two testaments and rearranged the order of the books.
   c. Rearranged the order of the New Testament books and separated the two testaments.
   d. Removed the Old Testament from the Bible and kept only the New Testament.

5. What does the name Abram mean?

   a. Father of a multitude of nations
   b. Blameless father
   c. Exalted father
   d. Obedient father

6. What does the name Abraham mean?

   a. Father of a multitude of nations
   b. Blameless father
   c. Exalted father
   d. Obedient father

7. What is the significance of God's changing Abram's name to Abraham?

   a. So Abraham could become the father of the people of Israel
   b. God declared him worthy to inherit the birthright.
   c. So Abraham could initiate the line of patriarchs – Abraham, Isaac, Jacob and Joseph.
   d. So Abraham could walk before God and be blameless.

8. What does Noah's name mean?

   a. Remnant
   b. Righteous
   c. Blameless
   d. Rest

9. How does the number forty explain the purpose of the wilderness wandering after the Exodus from Egypt?

   a. God gave the law to Israel.
   b. God instructed Israel through a process of testing.
   c. This was a period of trial and chastisement for the purpose of selection.
   d. The incident of the golden calf led to God's decision as to who could enter the Promised Land.

10. When God delivered the Israelites into the hand of the Philistines for forty years (Judges 30:1), how was this event dramatically different from what would have been expected?

    a. The Philistines were the allies of the Israelites, not enemies.
    b. The number 20 is most commonly used in the Book of Judges, not the number 40.
    c. The judges delivered the Israelites from the hand of their enemies, so being delivered into the hand of the enemy would have been startling.
    d. Forty was connected with "rest" in preparation for the next attack by the enemy.

Chapter 7
Echoes in Scripture

Summary

We have spent the last six chapters, the first half of the course, working in the Hebrew Scriptures. It is now time to turn to the "New" Testament, which you will find is a form of commentary on the "Old," because it draws from the Hebrew text to explain the Messiah and all the events that surrounded him. In this chapter you will practice listening for "echoes" in the New Testament that stimulate a verse or passage in the Hebrew Scriptures.

Outline of Lecture

I.   Proof-text versus a citation that is NOT a proof-text

    A.   Proof-text

        1.   Mat 3:3 – John the Baptist

        2.   Compare citation with what it has cited

        3.   Prophecy fulfilled

    B.   Citation that is NOT a proof-text

        1.   Rom 11:26-17

        2.   Paul deleted most of verse 21

        3.   Meaning in the artistic handling of the citation

II.   Echo

    A.   Mat 18:6 echoes Lev 19:14

    B.   Higher principle

III.   Echo in Romans 6

    A.   *"You are not under law but under grace"*

    B.   Context

        1.   Rom 6:1-10 (sin HAS been conquered)

        2.   Rom 6:11 (conclusion and introduction to what follows)

        3.   Rom 6:12-14 (words of warning includes *"you are no longer under law but under grace"*)

C. Echo — *"Sin shall not be master over you"* (Rom 6:14)

    a. Cain and Abel story — Echo is in Gen 4:7

    ROMANS: *Sin shall not be <u>master over you</u>,*
                  for you are not under law but under grace. (Rom 6:14)

    ....

    GENESIS: *If you do well, will not your countenance be lifted up? And if you do not do*
                 well, <u>sin</u> is crouching at the door; and its desire is for you, but <u>you must</u>
                 <u>*it*</u>. (Gen 4:7)

    b. Compare Paul's echo in Romans with what he has cited in the Cain and Abel story.

    c. Who will be the boss?

        1) Romans — *"Don't let sin be master over you"* (sin is the boss BUT we can now

             submit to grace and let God be the boss)

        2) Genesis — *"We must be master over sin"* (you are the boss)

    d. Review

D. How the echo operates

    1. Review Gen 4:1-4

    2. Contrast ("but") in Gen 4:4-5

        a. Abel's offering was accepted

        b. Cain's offering was NOT accepted

    3. Gen 4:5-6

        Cain became very angry and his <u>countenance fell</u>.
        Then the LORD said to Cain, "Why are you angry? And why has your <u>countenance</u>
             <u>*fallen*</u>*?*
        If you do well, will not your countenance be <u>lifted up</u>? (Gen 4:6-7)

        a. Repetition — countenance, fall

        b. Key word — "lifted up" = שאת (*se'eth*), exalted

        c. Italics have been added by the translators; take them out when you read.

        d. Double meaning of שאת

            1) Lift up (physically)

2) Exalted (lifted up)

e. "do well" = טוֹב do "good"

E. Imagery

> *Sin is crouching at your door; its desire is for you.* (Gen 4:7)

1. Imagery of a lion

2. You must master sin

F. Returning to Romans 6:12-14

> *"Do not let sin <u>reign</u> in your mortal body so that you obey its lusts."* (Rom 6:12)

1. Reign = rule, be master over

2. Question: Who is going to be the master?

G. Romans 6:13 – chiastic

> *Do not go on presenting the <u>members</u> of your body to sin as <u>instruments</u> of unrighteousness;*
> > *<u>but</u> present yourselves to God as those alive from the dead,*
> *and your <u>members</u> as <u>instruments</u> of righteousness to God.* (Rom 6:13)

1. Two parallel lines – repetition of "members" and "instruments"

2. Sin was crucified with Yeshua on the cross

3. Alive from the dead (no sin)

H. Romans 6:15

> *For sin shall not be <u>master</u> over you,*
> *for you are not <u>under</u> law but <u>under</u> grace.*

1. "Master" = rule, reign, have dominion over

2. Repetition "under" - ὑπό (*hupo*)

3. "under [the control, authority] of law"

4. "under [the control, power, authority] of grace"

I. Now you can understand Romans 6:3

> *Do you not know that all of us who have been*
> > *baptized into Christ Jesus*
> > *have been baptized into His death?*
> *We have been buried with Him through baptism into death,*

SO THAT as Christ was raised from the dead through the glory of the Father, so we too might walk in newness of life. (Rom 6:3-4)

      1.   Key words – "baptize" (wash away sin), "buried" (into death with Yeshua)

      2.   Put sin to death in our lives

   J.   Now you can understand Romans 6:3

Words to be Defined

1.   Proof-text_____

_____

_____

2.   Citation_____

_____

_____

3.   Quotation_____

_____

_____

4.   שאת_____

_____

_____

Questions for Comprehension

1.   Why is Paul's citation in Romans 11:26-27 not a proof-text?_____

_____

_____

2.   What does it mean to see a verse in its context?_____

_____

_____

_____

3.   What is Paul echoing when he declares, *"sin shall not be master over you, for you are not under law but under grace"* (Rom 6:14)?_____

_____

_____

_____

_____

4. In the linguistic structure of Romans 6:1-14, there are three parts. What are the three parts, and what function is each part playing? _____

_____

_____

_____

_____

_____

_____

5. What is the imagery in *"sin is crouching at your door,"* which we see in Genesis 4:7? _____

_____

_____

_____

_____

_____

6. In the following verse, what word has a double meaning, and how is this word used as a "play on words"? *"If you do well will not your countenance be lifted up?"* _____

_____

_____

_____

_____

_____

7. What is the meaning of "baptize" in the following verse, and how does this word contribute to the meaning of Paul's message? *"Do you not know that all of us who have been baptized into Christ Jesus have been baptized into His death?"* (Rom 6:3)_____

_____

_____

_____

_____

_____

Building Skills

1. It is VERY important that you memorize the Greek alphabet. There is a video lesson on http://bibleinteract.com that will help you do this. Once you learn the Greek alphabet you will be able to work with Greek New Testament words.

1. Dr. Davis heard an echo in Romans 6:14 of the Cain and Abel story, which was stimulated by the English translation, "master over." *"Sin shall not be master over you, for you are not under law but under grace."* You have learned that you cannot rely on English translations for a depth of meaning. Furthermore, you must let your curiosity draw you to key words that you can then look up in http://www.biblos.com. "Master over" is such a key word.

   a. In biblos.com find Romans 6:14, and then identify the word that has been translated with Strong's number 2961. Ordinarily I tell you *not* to look at Strong's definition but to go directly to the verses in which the Greek word appears. However, in this case you should take time to examine the information that Strong offers (note that κυριεύω is in a verbal form). What is Strong's definition?_____

   _____

   _____

   b. Next, look below Strong's definition at "Word Studies." Biblos offers "Word Studies" only for the New Testament. The authors of the website have conducted their own search of the Greek word in all the verses where it appears in the NT, and have offered their sense of meaning from this "word study." How does Strong's definition compare with the result of the "word study"?_____

   _____

   _____

   _____

   _____

   _____

   c. Next, note in the "word study" that the verbal form κυριεύω comes from the noun κύριος. Click on Strong's number 2962 to find the noun κύριος. From Strong's definition of κύριος, what does this noun mean?_____

   _____

   _____

   _____

   _____

   d. You are now on the page for the noun, κύριος. Look at the right column that lists all the verses that contain κύριος (when you reach the bottom of the right column, click on 722 occurrences to view the entire list of verses). On your own scratch paper at home, make a list that identifies the 17 verses in Mark that contain κύριος (Mark 12:29 will be listed twice). You will find that the word can be used in three different ways – for God the

Father, for His son the Messiah, and in a general sense as a person with authority over others. Read each of the 17 verses in Mark in their context and mark on your list how κύριος is used. Then fill in the chart below.

How κύριος is used in the Gospel of Mark	
	Number of times
God the Father	
His son the Messiah	
A person with authority over others	

Questions for Discussion

1. Paul declares, *"You are not under law but under grace"* (Rom 6:14). A key word is "under," meaning "under the authority of." The Greek word is ὑπό, pronounced *hupo*. The Hebrew equivalent is תחת (*tachath*). This is a simple preposition that usually means physically under something. However, sometimes it is used in a metaphorical sense that stimulates vivid imagery. Consider the imagery and the metaphorical meaning of תחת and ὑπό in the following verses:

    Exodus 6:6-7
    Judges 3:30
    Psalm 8:6
    Psalm 91:4
    Matthew 23:37

2. Re-read Romans 6:1-4, which is rich with artistic nuances of the language.

    a. How did we die to sin?_____

    _____

    _____

    b. What does it mean to be "baptized into Christ Jesus?"_____

    _____

    _____

    _____

    c. What does it mean to be "baptized into his death?"_____

    _____

    _____

    _____

d. How have we been "buried with Christ through baptism into death?"_____
_____
_____
_____
_____
_____
_____

e. According to Paul, how can we walk in "newness of life"?_____
_____
_____
_____
_____
_____
_____

f. How has our "old self been crucified with Christ?"_____
_____
_____
_____
_____
_____
_____

g. What does it mean to be a "slave to sin"?_____
_____
_____
_____
_____
_____
_____

h. How can we be freed from sin?_____
_____
_____
_____
_____
_____
_____

Challenge Yourself!

Now that you know that baptism symbolically washes away sins, you are ready to consider the three baptisms in Matthew 3:11. What do you think these three baptisms are? (To learn more about the baptism by fire, you might want to do a word study on "fire.") _____

_____

_____

_____

_____

_____

_____

_____

_____

_____

_____

_____

Application Questions

1. Imagine that someone has accused you of "putting yourself back under the law because you were studying the Old Testament." How would you answer this accusation? _____

_____

_____

_____

_____

_____

_____

_____

_____

_____

_____

_____

_____

_____

_____

2. Do you know Christians whose worldly behavior warrants their being put back under the law? Give examples. More important, do you know Christians who have submitted to the authority of God's grace? Give examples. What is the difference between these two groups of people? To which group do you belong?_____

_____

_____

_____

_____

_____

_____

_____

_____

_____

_____

_____

_____

_____

_____

Chapter 7 Quiz

1. What is a proof text?
    a. a citation
    b. an echo
    c. an allusion
    d. prophecy fulfilled

2. What is an allusion?
    a. a citation
    b. an echo
    c. a implicit reference to Scripture
    d. prophecy fulfilled

3. How can one see, in the NASB, a citation of the Hebrew Scriptures in the New Testament?
    a. The citation appears in red letters
    b. The citation appears in capital letters
    c. The citation appears in italics
    d. The citation is underlined

4. Romans 6:1-14 is divided into three parts with a transition verse between the parts.
    a. True
    b. False

5. We are alerted to an echo in Romans 6:14 by what word or phrase?
    a. sin
    b. master over
    c. under law
    d. under grace

6. Why did God accept Abel's offering?
    a. The offering was the first fruit of his flock
    b. He gave the fat portion to burn as sweet incense to God
    c. He gave the best of what he had
    d. All of the above

7. The passage uses word-play to convey the manner in which Cain can offer himself to God in an acceptable way.
    a. True
    b. False

8. Those who are under God's grace are free from any rules and authority.
    a. True
    b. False

9. Paul declares in Romans 6:3 that we have been baptized into the resurrection of Christ.
    a. True
    b. False

10. According to Paul, death no longer has dominion over those who belong to God.
    a. True
    b. False

Chapter 8
Word Study

Summary

After your curiosity leads you to a key word in a verse or passage, you should look up the original word (rather than relying on the English translation). Then you can conduct a word study of where the original word appears in Scripture and how it is used in each verse.

Outline of Lecture

I.   Review the use of http://biblos.com

II.   Look for a pattern

    A.   First usage of a word is always significant

    B.   List verses in the order in which a word appears in Scripture

    C.   Look for a pattern

III. Inductive versus deductive thinking

    A.   Inductive

    B.   Deductive

IV.   Romans 12:1-2

> *I urge you, brethren, by the mercies of God, to present your bodies a living and holy sacrifice, acceptable to God, which is your spiritual service of worship.*
>
> *And do not be conformed to this world, but be transformed by the renewing of your mind, so that you may prove what the will of God is, that which is good and acceptable and perfect.* (Rom 12:1-2)

    A.   Key words

        1.   Conformed

        2.   Transformed - μεταμορφόω

            a.   Mat 17:2 (transfigured)

            b.   Mark 9:2 (transfigured)

            c.   Rom 12:2 (transformed)

            d.   2 Co 3:18 (transformed)

B. Mat 17:2; Mk 9:2

   1. Transfiguration of Yeshua

   2. Face shone like the sun; garments became as white as light

   3. Symbolism of sun and light

   4. Prophetic future – sun no longer set; everlasting light (Is 60:20)

C. Rom 12:2

   1. μεταμορφόω means "to change"

   2. renewing your mind

D. 2 Co 3:18

   We all, with unveiled face, beholding as in a mirror the glory of the Lord, are being transformed into the same image from glory to glory, just as from the Lord, the Spirit. (2 Co 3:18

   1. See ourselves as God sees us

   2. Veil separated the priests from the Holy of Holies

   3. We are becoming the glory of God

   4. How does God see you

   5. The Hebraic sense of time

V. Presentation of "metamorphosis" as a metaphor for the Christian life

A. Start with a seed

B. Ugly caterpillar – shaped by the world

C. Wrapped in a cocoon – immersed in the Word of God and growing relationship with Yeshua

D. Beautiful butterfly – a new creation

Words to be Defined

1. μεταμορφόω_____

   _____

   _____

2. Metamorphosis_____

_____

_____

3. Transfigured_____

_____

_____

Questions for Comprehension

1. What is the difference between inductive and deductive thinking? _____

_____

_____

_____

_____

_____

2. What does the word μεταμορφόω mean? How is the word used in the account of the transfiguration of Yeshua? How is it used in Romans? How is it used in 2 Corinthians?_____

_____

_____

_____

_____

_____

_____

3. How is the transfiguration of Yeshua prophetic?_____

_____

_____

_____

_____

_____

4. How does Paul tell us to "change"? _____

_____

_____

_____

_____

_____

_____

5. In 2 Corinthians 3:18 we are to change "from glory to glory." What is the first "glory"? What is the second "glory"?_____

_____

_____

_____

_____

_____

_____

_____

_____

6. What is the process of metamorphosis of a caterpillar, and how does this help us understand Romans 12:1-2?_____

_____

_____

_____

_____

_____

_____

_____

_____

_____

_____

Building Skills

1. In 1 Thessalonians 5:6 you will find a word that has been translated "sober" (NASB, KJV).

    a. Use http://biblos.com to identify the Greek word._____

    b. List below the six verses where this Greek word appears in the New Testament._____

    _____

    _____

    _____

    _____

    c. Read each verse in its context and, in the chart below, write a brief note to explain how the word is used in each verse.

    d. All of these verses have one topic in common, which is a theme or pattern. Describe this pattern at the bottom of the chart.

Verse	Brief Notes
1.	
2.	
3.	
4.	
5.	
6.	
Pattern:	

Questions for Discussion

1. How can we be a living and holy sacrifice? Give some examples. How is this your spiritual service of worship? Are there other ways that you can worship the Lord? _____

   _____

   _____

   _____

   _____

   _____

   _____

2. How does looking at the Lord Yeshua (metaphorically in a mirror) help us change into the image of God? How does the answer to this question prompt changes in your own life?_____

   _____

   _____

   _____

3. Read Matthew 17:1-13 and Mark 9:2-13 about the transfiguration of Yeshua. These two parallel accounts are teeming with symbols that have become metaphors, echoes from the Hebrew Scriptures, key words that simulate your curiosity, and startling language that will lead you to deeper meaning.
    a. Start by filling in the chart below.
    b. Then pose a list of questions that the passage precipitates in your mind.
    c. Do your best to answer your questions.

	Matthew 17:1-13	Mark 9:2-13	Notes
Symbol			
Metaphor			
Echo			
Key Word			
Vivid Imagery			
Strange or Startling			

Questions	Answers

Read Matthew 18:6-10. This passage is filed with vivid imagery, incisive symbolism, and a lot of hyperbole (extreme exaggeration that makes a point).

1. Start by looking at the echo in Leviticus 19:14. What is the higher principle that Yeshua is teaching?_____
    _____
    _____
    _____

2. Next it is time to look at images and symbols. What is a mill stone? Can you find a picture of one on the internet? How is Mat 18:6 using the mill stone as hyperbole? What point is Yeshua making with the mill stone?_____
    _____
    _____
    _____
    _____

3. In verses 8-9, how is making *yourself* blind or lame a form of irony on the law in Leviticus 19:14?_____
    _____
    _____
    _____
    _____
    _____

4. "Fiery hell" is the Greek γέενναν τοῦ πυρός. When you learn your Greek alphabet you will be able to see that this is "the fire of Gehenna." Gehenna refers to the Hinnom Valley just south of Jerusalem where the garbage and refuse was burned. Use your Bible atlas to see where the Hinnom Valley is located.

5. How is "the fire of Gehenna" a metaphor for punishment?_____
    _____
    _____
    _____
    _____
    _____

Application Questions

3. Are you an inductive or deductive thinker? Give some examples to support your answer. As an inductive or deductive thinker, how do you conduct your Bible study?._____

_____

_____

_____

_____

_____

_____

_____

_____

_____

_____

_____

_____

_____

_____

_____

_____

4. How has the world conformed you to its image? Give some specific examples. What have you been successful in changing? Explain how you accomplished this, which can be a witness for others._____

_____

_____

_____

_____

_____

_____

_____

_____

_____

_____

_____

_____

_____

_____

_____

_____

Chapter 8 Quiz

1. What is the primary purpose of an interlinear Bible?
   a. Link to Strong's concordance.
   b. Provide a word for word reference from the English translation to the original Greek or Hebrew word
   c. Offer a list of verses where the original Hebrew or Greek word appears in Scripture.
   d. All of the above.

2. Deductive thinking focuses on the details.
   a. True
   b. False

3. What is the primary purpose of a word study?
   a. Give a plain and simple definition of the word.
   b. Identify the original word that has been translated into English.
   c. Read each verse in its context.
   d. Derive a depth of understanding of the original word.

4. How do you identify a key word in a verse or passage?
   a. Let your curiosity draw you to a key word.
   b. The key word will likely be a verb because verbs are the main carriers of meaning.
   c. The key word will likely be an adjective because adjectives are descriptive.
   d. None of the above.

5. What is an echo?
   a. A citation from the Hebrew Scriptures
   b. An allusion to the Hebrew Scriptures
   c. A verse or passage from the Hebrew Scriptures
   d. None of the above

6. In Romans 12:1, what does Paul claim is your spiritual service of worship?
   a. Prayer
   b. Walking as Yeshua walked
   c. Becoming a living sacrifice
   d. Doing the works of righteousness

7. What does the Greek word μεταμορφόω mean?
   a. Trust in God
   b. Love of Christ
   c. Be changed
   d. Be enlightened

8. In the Hebraic sense of time, when does God create righteousness in His children?
   a. When they first belong to Him
   b. At some time in the future
   c. In our lives today when we walk in the ways of God
   d. All of the above

9. In 2 Co 3:18, Paul declares that God's children are being transformed from glory to glory. What is the first glory?
   a. God has created us in His own image
   b. Yeshua the Messiah is the first glory in whom we believe
   c. God the Father is the first glory
   d. None of the above

10. In 2 Co 3:18, Paul declares that God's children are being transformed from glory to glory. What is the second glory?
   a. We become the glory of God when we first believe in His son
   b. We will become the glory of God at some time in the future when He gives us eternal life
   c. We become the glory of God when we walk as Yeshua walked
   d. None of the above

Chapter 9
Unraveling and Chiastic Construction

Summary

Chiasm is a literary device that was in common use throughout the ancient Near East, and is quite prevalent in Scripture. Chiasm uses parallel lines on either side of a chiastic center. You will often find an intriguing relationship between the parallel lines as well as a penetrating relationship between the parallel lines and the central thought of the chiasm.

Outline of Lecture

I.   Chiasm

   A. Parallel lines - relationship

   B. Chiastic center

II.   Parallel lines

   A. Psalm 6:1-2

   > *O LORD,*
   >   *Do not <u>rebuke</u> me in Your <u>anger</u>,*
   >   *Nor <u>chasten</u> me in Your <u>wrath</u>.*
   > *Be <u>gracious</u> to me, O LORD,*
   >   *for I am <u>pining away</u>;*
   > *<u>Heal</u> me, O LORD,*
   >   *for my bones are <u>dismayed</u>.*

III. Chiastic structure

   A. ABA

   B. ABCDCBA

      A. Man

         B. Woman

            C. Child of God

         B. Woman from the rib of man

      A. Man created by God

IV.   Chiasm – Luke 15:19-21

> *I am <u>no longer </u>worthy to be called your son; make me as one of your hired men.*
>> *He <u>got up</u> and came to his father. But while he was still a long way off,*
>>> *His father saw him and <u>felt</u> compassion for him, and <u>ran</u> and embraced him and <u>kissed</u> him.*
>> *Father, I have sinned against heaven and in your sight; I am <u>no longer worthy to be called your son</u>.*

1. Relationship between the parallel lines

2. First "no longer worthy" – sees himself as unworthy

3. Second "no longer worthy" - repents

4. Chiastic Center – the father's response to his son when he "stood"

The son's response to the father was to "repent"

IV.   A Puzzling Passage – Romans 10:9-10

A. Several possible interpretations

> *If you <u>confess</u> with your <u>mouth</u> Jesus as Lord,*
>> *and <u>believe in your heart</u> that God raised Him from the dead,*
>>> *you will be <u>saved</u>;*
>> *for <u>with the heart</u> a person <u>believes</u>, resulting in righteousness,*
> *and with the <u>mouth</u> he <u>confesses</u>, resulting in <u>salvation</u>.*

1. Listen for repetition

2. Questions

    a. Are there one or two requirements to be saved?

    b. What does the heart and mouth symbolize?

B. Something puzzling about "saved" and "salvation" – not in parallel

1. Hebraic sense of time

    a. 2 Peter 3:8

    b. Not linear, God created time and is in time

    c. Only two sense of time – complete and incomplete

    d. Genesis 2:2 – completion was complete in the beginning

    e. Genesis 1:27 = In the beginning God created perfection and righteousness

f. Timeline

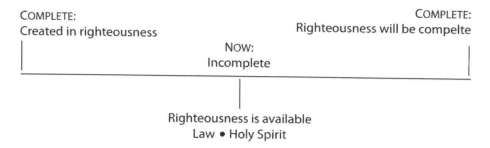

Hebraic Sense of Time
Two Aspects of Righteousness

COMPLETE:
Created in righteousness

COMPLETE:
Righteousness will be compelte

NOW:
Incomplete

Righteousness is available
Law • Holy Spirit

2. What does it mean to be "saved" or "rescued"?

a. Two aspects of salvation

   1) Belong to God – Passover narrative (saved by promise)

   2) Daily rescue from bondage to the world – parting of the Red Sea

Hebraic Sense of Time
Two Aspects of Salvation

God sees you
as righteousness (saved)

You will be righteous
(saved)

1. Saved by promise
2. Walk in wholenss

NOW

C. Returning to Romans 10:9-10 (ABCBA chiastic construction)

   1. Chiastic center – two aspects of salvation

   2. B lines

      a. Believe in your heart

      b. First aspect of salvation (promise of eternal life)

      c. You are righteous in God's eyes and belong to Him

   3. A lines

a. "resulting in salvation" is parallel with "confess with your mouth Jesus *as* Lord" (second aspect of salvation)

b. Submitting to Yeshua as Lord is the second aspect of salvation

Words to be Defined

1. Chiasm_____

_____

_____

2. ABA Construction_____

_____

_____

3. ABCDCBA Construction_____

_____

_____

4. Hebraic Sense of Time_____

_____

_____

5. Two Aspects of Salvation_____

_____

_____

Questions for Comprehension

1. What makes two lines parallel in the biblical text? _____

_____

_____

2. Where is the main point of a chiastic construction?_____

_____

_____

3. Where are the relationships in a chiastic construction?_____

_____

_____

_____

4. In Luke 15:19-21, what was the relationship of the A lines? What did the chiastic center convey? _____

_____

_____

_____

_____

5. What are the two aspects of salvation? _____

_____

_____

_____

_____

_____

6. In Romans 10:9-10, you saw that the chiastic center pointed to two aspects of salvation. How do the B lines convey the first aspect of salvation? How do the A lines convey the second aspect of salvation? ____

_____

_____

_____

_____

_____

_____

7. How is the Hebraic sense of time different from our Greek, modern, western sense of time? _____

_____

_____

_____

_____

_____

Building Skills

1. Consider the following chiastic structure in Galatians 2:16.

> A. *Not justified by works of the Law*
>> B. *Justified by faith in Christ Jesus*
>>> C. *We have believed in Christ Jesus*
>> B. *We may be justified by faith in Christ Jesus*
> A. *Not justified by works of the Law*

a. What is the relationship between each pair of parallel lines (A and B) in this chiastic construction? ____
_____
_____

b. What is the relationship between all the parallel lines and the chiastic center?_____
_____
_____

c. From your examination of the relationships between the parallel lines, and the relationship between the parallel lines and the chiastic center, what do you think is the depth of meaning that this chiasm conveys?_____
_____
_____
_____
_____

2. Consider the following chiastic structure in Romans 11:18-20.

    A. *Do not be arrogant toward the branches*
        B. *The root supports you*
            C. *Branches were broken off*
                D. *I might be grafted in*
            C. *Broken off for their unbelief*
        B. *You stand by your faith*
    A. *Do not be conceited*

a. What is the relationship between each pair of parallel lines (A, B, C) in this chiastic construction?_____
_____
_____

b. What is the relationship between all the parallel lines and the chiastic center?_____
_____
_____
_____
_____

c. From your examination of the relationships between the parallel lines, and the relationship between the parallel lines and the chiastic center, what do you think is the depth of meaning that this chiasm conveys?_____
_____
_____
_____
_____

Questions for Discussion

1. It is very important that you understand the two aspects of salvation, so you need to discuss this at some length. Here are some questions you might wish to consider.

   a. What has been your traditional understanding of "who will be saved?" How did you come to this understanding?_____

   _____

   _____

   _____

   _____

   _____

   _____

   b. Are you aware of other possible theological interpretations of "who will be saved?" If so, explain.___

   _____

   _____

   _____

   _____

   _____

   c. What is the Greek sense of time, and how does that lead to certain interpretations of "who will be saved"?_____

   _____

   _____

   _____

   _____

   d. What is the Hebraic sense of time, and how does that explain Genesis 1:27?_____

   _____

   _____

   _____

   _____

   e. In the Hebraic sense of time, what is the relationship between God's creation in the beginning and the End of Time?_____

   _____

   _____

   _____

   _____

   _____

2. Draw a timeline and label it, "Hebraic Sense of Time." Where would you put the following on your timeline? (Remember, this is the HEBRAIC sense of time.)

   a. The day you were born_____
   _____
   _____
   _____

   b. The day you first belonged to God_____
   _____
   _____
   _____

   c. You are standing in righteousness before the righteous God_____
   _____
   _____
   _____

   d. A moment in time when you are walking in perfection without sin_____
   _____
   _____
   _____

   e. A time when you are always walking in perfection without sin_____
   _____
   _____
   _____

   f. You commit some sin_____
   _____
   _____
   _____

   g. You are "one" with God_____
   _____
   _____
   _____

   h. God created you in His image_____
   _____
   _____
   _____

i.   God sees you as righteous_____

_____

_____

_____

3.   You have worked the chiastic structure in Galatians 2:16.

   a.   Now read this verse in its context. What verses comprise the context?_____

   _____

   _____

   b.   Who are the "we" in Gal 2:15? These are the ones that Paul is addressing in Gal 2:16._____

   _____

   _____

   _____

   _____

   _____

   c.   How does the chiastic center instruct those thate Paul refers to as "we"?_____

   _____

   _____

   _____

   _____

   d.   How does Paul's instruction apply to us today?_____

   _____

   _____

   _____

   _____

Challenge Yourself!

4.   You have also worked the chiastic structure in Romans 11:18-20. Pose your own questions for this chiasm, and discuss the answers._____

_____

_____

_____

_____

_____

_____

Application Questions

1. Dr. Davis suggested that God sees you as righteous when you first belong to Him, and she pointed to Genesis 1:27. This understanding is quite different from the theological interpretation that we are born under sin, are sinners at heart, and need to be instructed and guided to become what God wants us to be. Thus, we have two conflicting perceptions of how God is working with mankind. If God has created righteousness in us, how does that affect our daily walk with God, and what is the role of the Holy Spirit?

   _____
   _____
   _____
   _____
   _____
   _____
   _____
   _____
   _____
   _____
   _____
   _____
   _____

2. Review Luke 15:19-21.

   a. What are the three steps conveyed in this chiasm? HINT: The first step is in the first A line. The second step is in the chiastic center. The third and final is in the second A line._____
   _____
   _____
   _____
   _____

   b. How is the relationship between the two A lines cause and effect?_____
   _____
   _____
   _____

   c. How does the chiastic center lead to the effect in the second A line?_____
   _____
   _____
   _____

3. Now you are ready to apply this understanding of Luke 15:19-21 to your life.

   a. What are some examples of the first A line part of your life?_____

      _____

      _____

      _____

      _____

      _____

      _____

      _____

      _____

      _____

      _____

   b. How has God worked in your life that is conveyed by the chiastic center?_____

      _____

      _____

      _____

      _____

      _____

      _____

      _____

      _____

      _____

      _____

   c. What are some example of the second A line part of your life? How did God operate to bring this about?_____

      _____

      _____

      _____

      _____

      _____

      _____

      _____

      _____

      _____

Chapter 9 Quiz

1. Parallel lines are always connected by the same or similar words.
   a. True
   b. False

2. The Book of Psalms is written completely in Hebraic poetry.
   a. True
   b. False

3. Chiasm is a unique linguistic device that appears only in Scripture.
   a. True
   b. False

4. Chiasm is constructed by using parallel lines that point to a chiastic center.
   a. True
   b. False

5. There are two lines in the chiastic center of Luke 15:19-21 about the prodigal son.
   a. True
   b. False

6. The message of salvation in Scripture deals exclusively with salvation from death to life through faith in Yeshua the Messiah.
   a. True
   b. False

7. There are two aspects of salvation in Scripture.
   a. True
   b. False

8. Romans 10:9-10 declares that a person is saved from death to life if he/she believes in his or her heart that God raised Yeshua from the dead.
   a. True
   b. False

9. Romans 10:9-10 declares that a person must first believe that God raised Yeshua from the dead and then must confess Yeshua as Lord in order to be saved from death to life.
   a. True
   b. False

10. The second aspect of salvation allows us to live in harmony with God in our lives today.
    a. True
    b. False

Chapter 10
What to do with a Citation

Summary

There are over 300 citations in the New Testament that quote the Old Testament. We used to think these citations were all proof-texts, which proved that a prophecy in the Old Testament had been fulfilled by God's son Yeshua. Furthermore, when the citation differed from what it was citing, many scholars believed that the New Testament text had been composed from different sources. Dr. Davis has come to a different conclusion.

Outline of Lecture

I.   Homework: Chiasm of Galatians 2:16

      A.   Context is using irony

          1.   "We *are* Jews nature by nature

          2.   The chiastic center says "we" have believed in Yeshua.

          3.   The "we" is referring to the Jews in verse 15. That is, they are believers in Yeshua with the gift of the Holy Spirit.

      B.   Parallel lines moving away from the chiastic center.

          1.   B lines are closest to the center.

          2.   Through faith in Christ they have been made righteous.

      C.   Moving away from the chiastic center.

          1.   "Studying" and "knowing" the law doesn't make you righteous.

          2.   "Walking" in the law by the gift of the Holy Spirit will make you righteous.

II.   Citation in the Parable of the Mustard Seed

      A.   Citation in capital letters; location of citation in middle margin (Ez 17:23)

      B.   Something strange and puzzling – Mustard seed does not become a trees

      C.   What to do with a citation

          1.   Find the cited verse in the Hebrew Scriptures

          2.   Identify the context (likely memorized block). Read aloud and "listen."

          3.   Compare the NT verse with what it cites in the Hebrew Scriptures.

4. Anything startling? Additions? Deletions? Changes?

5. Return to the NT verse.

D. Ezekiel 17:22-23

E. רוּם (*rum*) – high, exalted

F. .Compare NT citation with what it has cited in Ezekiel

And birds of every kind will nest under it; they will nest in the shade of its branches.   Ez 17:22-23

The mustard seed *"becomes a tree, so that the birds of the air come and nest in its branches."*
Mat 13:32

G. What the ancient listeners would have heard (intentional changes).

1. I will pluck from the topmost a tender one and plant it on a high mountain (exalted ones on Mt. Zion)

2. It [tender, exalted one] will bear fruit.

3. Birds will nest in the shade of its branches. *Olam haba*

4. NOW birds will nest in its branches.

H. Who will bear fruit for God?

1. Disciples (followers)

2. Servants

3. The Remnant

I. Who is walking in the Kingdom of God? (now)

J. Who will nest in the branches? (future)

III. Citation in Ephesians 4:8

Therefore it says, WHEN HE ASCENDED ON HIGH, HE LED CAPTIVE A HOST OF CAPTIVES AND HE GAVE GIFTS TO MEN. (Eph 4:8 citing Ps 68:18)

A. Context in Ephesians – disciples are servants of God.

"I, the prisoner of the Lord, implore you to walk in a manner worthy of the calling with which you have been called." (Eph 4:1)

B. Find the cited verse in its context (context of Psalm 68:18)

   1. Mount of God

   2. Dwelling place of God

   3. Thousands upon thousands of chariots (future battle)

   4. "You have ascended on high. You have led captive *Your* captives. Play on words – disciples are servants who have been led into captivity in service to God.

   5. You have received gifts among men." *Olam haba* – nations bring gifts to God's people.

C. Compare the NT verse with what it cites in the Hebrew Scriptures. Anything startling? Additions? Deletions? Changes?

   1. Ps 68:18 – received gifts (future)

   2. Eph 4:8 – giving gifts (now) – Eph 4:11-12

Words to be Defined

1. Mustard plant in Israel_____

   _____

   _____

2. *Olam haba*_____

   _____

   _____

3. Disciple_____

   _____

   _____

Questions for Comprehension

1. How do you know when a NT author is citing from the Hebrew Scriptures? _____

   _____

2. How do you find what the NT author has cited?_____

   _____

   _____

3. The first thing you must do is to read the NT citation in its context in the New Testament. What is the next thing you do?_____

_____

_____

4. You should read the citation (in its context) aloud. What are you listening for? _____

_____

_____

5. What is the purpose of comparing the NT passage with what it has cited in the Hebrew Scriptures?_____

_____

_____

_____

6. Why is the "mustard tree" startling?_____

_____

_____

_____

7. When comparing Ephesians 4:8 with what it has cited in Psalm 68:18, what has the author of Ephesians changed? What meaning results?_____

_____

_____

_____

_____

Building Skills

Challenge Yourself!

Carefully consider Paul's citation of Habakkuk 2:4 in Romans 1:17.

1. Identify and summarize the immediate context of the citation in Romans._____

_____

_____

_____

2. Now turn to the book of Habakkuk, which appears to have two parts. There is the oracle which Habakkuk saw in chapters 1-2, and a prayer of Habakkuk in chapter 3. You will now work on chapters 1-2 where the citation is located. What is the main theme of the oracle?___

_____

_____

3. Now break the oracle into its parts, and identify the main theme of the following parts – 1:1-4; 1:5-11 (the Chaldeans are the Babylonians who took the two southern tribes of Judah and Benjamin into captivity); 1:12-17; 2:1-4; 2:5-8; 2:9-17; 2:18-20._____

_____

_____

_____

4. Note that these seven parts are in a chiastic construction. Write a few words as a brief description beside each letter.

    A.

        B.

            C

                D.

            C.

        B.

    A.

5. The cited verse is in the chiastic center.

6. Now compare Romans 1:17 (in its immediate context) to Habakkuk 2:4 (in its context of the oracle in which it appears). Consider the time for each. Habakkuk 2:4 seems to be pointing forward to a time of future judgment. However, Romans 1:17 refers to the first coming of Yeshua when God gave His son, and through faith in His son the gift of the Holy Spirit, to those with faith in Yeshua the Messiah. How does Romans 1:17 suggest that the prophecy of Habakkuk has been fulfilled in part, but its final fulfillment is still future?_____

_____

_____

_____

7. Now consider "from faith to faith." Dr. Davis has suggested that God sees His children as righteous when they first belong to Him (righteous without sin as a newborn baby is perfect). In a metaphorical sense, all God's children have righteousness in them because they belong to God. But then, God instructs them to walk in that righteousness. And ultimately, at some future time God will have drawn all His children to Him in a righteous condition so they can come into His presence without death that sin accomplishes. With these thoughts in mind, what is the meaning of "from faith to faith"?_____

_____

_____

_____

_____

Questions for Discussion

1. Who is God leading into captivity? How is He doing this? For what purpose? _____
   _____
   _____
   _____
   _____

2. Do your own work to compare the Parable of the Mustard Seed with what it has cited in Ezekiel. You may be surprised by what you see. It may or may not be what Dr. Davis has seen.

3. The author of Ephesians refers to himself as a "prisoner of the Lord."

   a. What does it mean that he is a prisoner of the Lord?_____
      _____
      _____
      _____
      _____

   b. In Ephesians 4:1 we read, "I, the prisoner of the Lord, implore you to walk in a manner worthy of the calling with which you have been called," Why is this calling NOT to believe in Yeshua in order to belong to God? What exactly is this calling?_____
      _____
      _____
      _____
      _____
      _____

   c. We are called in more than one way. What are the other ways, in addition to your answer to number b. above, in which God calls His children?_____
      _____
      _____
      _____
      _____
      _____

   d. What does it mean to be "worthy"?_____
      _____
      _____
      _____
      _____
      _____

Application Questions

1. Do you know someone who is a disciple of Yeshua by his or her deep commitment to follow and obey? What has led you to this conclusion? Is this person a mentor in your life? Where are you in your life of discipleship?_____

   _____

   _____

   _____

   _____

   _____

   _____

   _____

   _____

   _____

   _____

   _____

   _____

2. How does the Parable of the Mustard seed give us a glimpse of the future in God's great plan of redemption? Does this glimpse of the future encourage you to walk in godly ways in your life today? Explain your answer._____

   _____

   _____

   _____

   _____

   _____

   _____

   _____

   _____

   _____

   _____

   _____

   _____

   _____

Chapter 10 Quiz

1. Why is Galatians 2:15 ironic?
   a. Paul was ridiculing the Jewish believers who were insisting of knowledge of the Law in order to please God.
   b. Paul was accusing the Jewish believers of pride in their knowledge of the Law.
   c. Paul was demonstrating that Jewish believers in Christ were no better than the Gentile believers.
   d. All of the above.

2. Galatians 2:16 is in what kind of a chiastic construction?
   a. ABA
   b. ABCBA
   c. ABBA
   d. ABCDCBA

3. Why can we deduce that the Jews in Galatia, who were insisting that the Gentile believers know the Law and be circumcised, were believers in Christ?
   a. Paul spoke to them with words of irony.
   b. Paul insisted that works of the Law could not make a person righteous.
   c. Paul declared that "we have believed in Christ."
   d. None of the above.

4. The parable of the mustard seed contains a citation of Isaiah 56:11.
   a. True
   b. False

5. When Dr. Davis instructed you to read a citation in its context in the Hebrew Scriptures, to what was she referring?
   a. the chapter in which the citation appears
   b. the verse in which the citation appears
   c. all the surrounding verses in which the citation appears
   d. the likely memorized block of verses

6. What is the actual size of a mustard plant in Israel?
   a. larger than the garden plants
   b. a tree
   c. a small plant
   d. none of the above

7. To what does the exalted top of the cedar refer?
   a. righteous ones
   b. those whom God is selecting as a remnant
   c. those whom God will plant on Mount Zion
   d. all of the above

8. Where do the cedar trees grow?
   a. Israel
   b. Syria
   c. Lebanon
   d. None of the above

9. Psalm 68:8 declares, "He led captive a host of captives." According to the author of Ephesians, who were the captives who were led captive?
    a. the children of Israel during their exodus from Egypt
    b. the righteous remnant
    c. those who believe in Yeshua the Messiah
    d. those who belong to God

10. In Ephesians 4:8, what are the "gifts"?
    a. eternal life
    b. a walk of righteousness
    c. the Lord Yeshua
    d. an ability to serve God

Chapter 11
One Unified Message

Summary

You have seen the intimate connection of the New Testament with the Hebrew Scriptures. As only one example there are over 300 citations in the New Testament that quote from the Hebrew Scriptures. There are also numerous allusions to the Hebrew Scriptures that imply a passage in the Hebrew text, as well as the frequency of Hebraic language patterns. This should not surprise you since the authors of the New Testament were, in large part, Jews who knew the Hebrew Scriptures by heart. Therefore, we can perceive the New Testament as a form of commentary on the Old.

Outline of Lecture

I.   Connecting the two testaments

    A.   Frequency of citations and allusions

    B.   Hebraic language patterns (parallel lines, idioms)

    C.   Hebrew words and concepts in the NT

    D.   Hebraic way of teaching (gives clues, not the answer)

    E.   NT is very Hebraic

II.   "God does not show partiality"

    A.   God is Israel's Father (Dt 32:6); Israel is His firstborn son (Ex 4:22)

    B.   No partiality – Dt 10:17; Acts 10:34

III.   God's great plan of redemption – one unified message (both testaments)

IV.   Two different perspectives

    A.   Jewish Perspective

        1.   Know they belong to God

        2.   Emphasis on daily living

    B.   Christian Perspective

        1.   Who will be saved?

        2.   God of the OT and God of the NT

C. Message of salvation requires a messiah – how? When?

V. God uses the language of judgment in the OT and the language of love in the NT. Same God. Different use of language.

    A. Language of judgment is for instruction

        1. Strict and stern words

        2. Turn away from sin to God

        3. Intense emotion

        4. Immediate urgency

        5. Goes back and forth between the carrot (future hope) and the stick (language of judgment

VI. Language of judgment in Isaiah 1:2-3

> *Sons I have reared and brought up,*
> > *But they have revolted against Me.*
> *An ox knows its owner,*
> *And a donkey its master's manger,*
> > *But Israel does not know,*
> > *My people do not understand.*

    A. Poetic rhythm (emotion)

    B. Parallel lines (meaning

    C. Vivid imagery – ox and donkey

    D. Irony – sarcasm, ridicule, humor

    E. Hyperbole – extreme exaggeration

        1. "revolted against me"

    F. Look for the message

        1. You do not know (the Torah)

        2. You do not understand (discern between good and evil) – using the Law

VII. Language of judgment in Matthew 18:-10

> *Whoever causes one of these little ones who believe in Me to stumble, it would be better for him to have a heavy millstone hung around his neck, and to be drowned in the depth of the sea.*

A. Context in the NT

    1. Yeshua is talking to disciples.

    2. They asked, "Who is greatest in the Kingdom of Heaven?"

    3. Answer requires extreme language

B. Imagery of a millstone – extreme exaggeration

    1. Message – higher principle

        a. "stumble" is an echo

        b. Disciples are to trying to elevate themselves (pride). They are stumbling and causing others to stumble

C. Imagery of fiery hell

    1. γέεννα (*gehenna*)

    2. Hinnom Valley where refuse was burned

    3. Dung Gate

VIII. Connecting the two testaments

A. Language of judgment in OT sounds like a God of judgment and wrath against the Jews.

B. Language of judgment is language of instruction from a loving Father

Words to be Defined

1. Partiality_____

_____

_____

2. Language of Judgment_____

_____

_____

3. Hyperbole_____

_____

_____

4. Millstone_____
_____
_____

5. Gehenna_____
_____
_____

6. Hinnom Valley_____
_____
_____

Questions for Comprehension

1. What does it mean that God shows no partiality? _____
_____
_____
_____
_____

2. How is the Hebraic way of teaching different from the way that we are typically taught today?_____
_____
_____
_____
_____

3. What are the reasons for Dr. Davis' conclusion that the New Testament is very Hebraic in its nature?_____
_____
_____
_____

4. What is the language of judgment? _____
_____
_____
_____
_____

5. How does Isaiah 1:2-3 use the language of judgment?_____
_____
_____
_____
_____

6. How does Matthew 18:1-10 use the language of judgment? _____
_____
_____
_____
_____

7. Why did Dr. Davis choose to teach on the language of judgment as a way to show the connection of the two testaments? _____
_____
_____
_____
_____

Building Skills

Challenge Yourself!

You will find an echo in Hebrews 3:5-6. If you are using a good reference Bible, you will see notes in the middle or bottom margin that identify echoes from other parts of Scripture. These will typically be small letters in the verse that relate to notes in the margin. It is vitally important that you learn how to see these echoes.

1. In the space below, list all the verses that are identified as echoes in Hebrews 3:5. _____
_____
_____
_____

2. Note that the echoes in verse 5 are almost exclusively from the Hebrew Scriptures. What do we learn about Moses from these echoes? _____
_____
_____
_____
_____

3. Note that the echoes in verse 6 are exclusively from the New Testament. Why do you think this is so? _____
_____
_____
_____
_____

4. Now consider the contrast between Moses in verse 5 and Yeshua in verse 6. The contrast is crafted around the concept of "how much more." Explain how much more Yeshua is with his "house" than Moses was with his "house." _____

_____

_____

_____

_____

Explain how Acts 2:14-21 connects the two testaments. What will you need to do to complete this exercise?

1. What is the context of Acts 2:14-21? _____

_____

2. Find the citation in the Hebrew Scriptures, and read it in its context.

3. Compare the NT citation with what it has cited.

4. Has anything been changed, added, deleted? _____

_____

_____

_____

5. What is the message that Peter was giving on the day of Pentecost? _____

_____

_____

_____

_____

_____

Questions for Discussion

1. What has been your traditional understanding about the relationship between the two testaments? Have you viewed the OT as a foundation for the new and better gospel? How and why does Dr. Davis disagree with this common understanding? What is your current thinking about the relationship between the two testaments? Explain your answer. _____

_____

_____

1. How is the parable in Matthew 21:33-41 connected to Isaiah's parable in Isaiah 5:1-7? I suggest you start in the NT passage first. Then work the parable in Isaiah before comparing the two.._____

   _____

   _____

   _____

2. To appreciate the account of the miracle of wine at Cana (John 2:1-10), you must first understand the significance of "new wine" in the Hebrew Scriptures. The first usage of the Hebrew word for "new wine" is in Genesis 27:28.

   a. What is the Hebrew word?_____

   b. How is this Hebrew word different from the most common word for wine?_____

      _____

   c. Conduct a word study in bblos.com for this Hebrew word that means "new wine".. Make a list of the verses, take brief notes about how the word is used in each verse, and look for a pattern of how the word is used._____

      _____

      _____

      _____

      _____

      _____

   d. Return to the NT account of the miracle at Cana. Discuss the significance of the new wine in this passage._____

      _____

      _____

      _____

      _____

   e. Now go back through John 2:1-10 to consider all the artistry of language.

   f. What is the message of this narrative account of Yeshua in Cana?_____

      _____

      _____

      _____

      _____

      _____

Application Questions

1. What has been your traditional understanding of hell? How does the imagery of the Hinnom Valley cause you to stop and ponder the meaning of "hell" in Scripture? How is the concept of hell a metaphor?_____

_____

_____

_____

_____

_____

_____

_____

_____

_____

_____

_____

_____

_____

_____

2. What has been your traditional understanding of how God is working with the children of Israel? A common interpretation is that all Jews must believe in God's son, Yeshua the Messiah. However, the question becomes when and how? What is your thinking about when and how? Give support for your answer (hopefully support from Scripture, not from what you have been taught)._____

_____

_____

_____

_____

_____

_____

_____

_____

_____

_____

_____

_____

_____

_____

Chapter 11 Quiz

1. How many citations of the Hebrew Scriptures are in the New Testament?
   a. More than 100
   b. More than 200
   c. More than 300
   d. None of the above

2. The New Testament is a kind of commentary on the Hebrew Scriptures.
   a. True
   b. False

3. God is not treating believers in Yeshua any differently than He has treated the children of Israel.
   a. True
   b. False

4. God uses stern and condemning language of judgment in both the Old Testament and the New Testament.
   a. True
   b. False

5. The God of the Old Testament is a God of wrath and judgment toward Israel whereas the God of the New Testament is quite different, a God of love and compassion toward believers in His son.
   a. True
   b. False

6. What is the figure of speech that uses extreme exaggeration?
   a. hendiadys
   b. homonym
   b. hyperbaton
   c. hyberbole

7. Irony often takes the form of ridicule.
   a. True
   b. False

8. When Yeshua used the imagery of a heavy millstone around a person's neck, to whom was he referring?
   a. Pharisees
   b. disciples
   c. Jews
   d. Christian believers

9. What was Yeshua's purpose when he said, "Pluck out your eye"?
   a. Instruction
   b. Condemnation
   c. Judgment
   d. None of the above

10. To what does "fiery hell" refer in Matthew 18:9?
    a. a place of eternal condemnation
    b. a place of punishment
    c. the dung gate in Jerusalem
    c. the Hinnom Valley outside of Jerusalem

Chapter 12
Stewards of the Mysteries of God

Summary

Throughout this course, you have been learning how to uncover a depth of meaning from Scripture which Yeshua called "mysteries." He declared that these mysteries were available to his disciples, who have made him Lord in their lives. Therefore, these disciples must become stewards of the mysteries. They must treasure them in their hearts, and you must use the mysteries as servants of the Lord Yeshua.

Outline of Lecture

I.   Servants and stewards

    A. Humility

    B. Penetrating a mystery – who are servants and stewards

       Let no one boast in men….
       You belong to Christ [Son]; and Christ belongs to God [Father].
       (1 Co 3:21,23)

    C. ὑμεῖς δὲ Χριστοῦ, Χριστὸς δὲ θεοῦ

       You are of Christ, Christ is of God

    D. Mysteries

       1. What is the relationship of the son to the Father?

       2. What is the relationship of believers to the son?

       3. What is the relationship of believers through the son to the Father?

II.   Review a metaphor

    A. Symbol

    B. Metaphor

       1. We eat the bread of life

       2. Everything about God is explained metaphorically

       3. Who is Christ? Who are we? Must be explained metaphorically

III.   "No man has seen God at any time" – Ex 33:20; John 3:18; 1 Tim 6:16

    A. God is in Christ (2 Co 5:19) - metaphor

1. separate but the Father is in the son

2. Christ speaks and acts for the Father

3. As God is Lord, so Yeshua is lord also.

4. The same metaphor is used for believers in Christ

B. Christ is in you (Col 1:27) – metaphor

1. Separate but Christ is in you

2. Disciples speak and act for the Messiah

C. Romans 10:9-10. Two aspects of salvation.

1. Those who belong to God are children of Israel and Gentile believers in Christ (first aspect)

2. Confess Yeshua as Lord; walk in wholeness

a. Disciple, follower of Christ

b. You are IN Christ and walk as he walked

c. You are one with Christ

IV.   Distinction between Christ in you and you in Christ

A. Christ in you

1. Gift from God

2. You belong to God with the promise of eternal life

B. You are in Christ

1. Speak for Christ

2. Walk as he walked

3. Do the works of Christ

4. Shine forth the light of God

V.   Christ is IN you (gift); you are IN Christ (walk)

A. Romans 8:10

B. Galatians 3:6

     C. 1 Corinthians 3:21-4:1

  VI.   Stewards over God's household

     A. 1 Colossians 1:25-27

          οἰκονομία (*oikonomia*)

          household - law

     B. Hebrews 3:6

     C. Romans 7:12

        1. νόμος (*nomos*)

        2. We help God's children walk in the ways of the Law

        3. בית אלהים (*house of God*)

Words to be Defined

1. Steward _____
_____
_____

2. Servant _____
_____
_____

3. Metaphor _____
_____
_____

4. οἰκονομία _____
_____
_____

Questions for Comprehension

1. Who are the stewards of the mysteries of God? _____
_____
_____
_____
_____
_____

2. Where are the mysteries of God?_____

_____

_____

_____

_____

_____

3. How do the stewards uncover these mysteries?_____

_____

_____

_____

_____

_____

4. What are they supposed to do with these mysteries? _____

_____

_____

_____

_____

_____

5. Who are the ones who are in God's household?_____

_____

_____

_____

_____

_____

Building Skills

1. Paul exhorts in his letter to the Corinthians, *"Let a man regard us in this manner, as servants of Christ and stewards of the mysteries of God"* (1 Co 3:21-4:1). In this chapter Dr. Davis helped you work on the concept of "steward." Now it is your turn to work on the concept of "servant." We have selected several NT verses for you to work through in the chart below. Remember to read each verse in its context, look up any key words, and identify artistic elements in the language.

Verse	Notes
Acts 3:26	
Acts 4:30	
1 Co 3:5	
2 Co 3:6	
Col 1:7	
Col 4:7	
1 Tim 4:6	

2. What are the requirements of a servant?_____

_____

_____

_____

_____

_____

3. Do you know any servants of Christ? What are their strengths? Do they have any weaknesses?_____

_____

_____

_____

_____

_____

_____

4. Are you a servant of the Lord Yeshua? Explain your answer._____

_____

_____

_____

_____

_____

_____

Questions for Discussion

1. Consider the parable in Luke 16:1-13, which is about faithful and unfaithful stewards or managers.

   a. You will find many artistic devices in this account, so work the parable carefully by first filling out the chart below.

Artistic language	Examples in Luke 16:1-13
Strange or startling	
Repetition	
Key words	
Symbols	
Irony	

b. Now it is time for you to start asking questions. Let your curiosity prompt these questions.

Questions	Discussion and answer

c. You are now ready to discuss the meaning of the parable._____
_____
_____
_____
_____
_____

2. We value your thoughts and suggestions, and use them to continue improving this program of teaching ancient methods of searching the Scriptures. Feel free to send us your thoughts on these and any other topics.

a. What did you learn?_____
_____
_____
_____
_____
_____
_____

b. What do you think are the strengths of this course?_____

_____

_____

_____

_____

_____

_____

_____

c. What are the weaknesses that need to be addressed?_____

_____

_____

_____

_____

_____

_____

_____

d. What advice would you give to other students who decide to take the course?_____

_____

_____

_____

_____

_____

_____

_____

e. Any other suggestions?_____

_____

_____

_____

_____

_____

_____

_____

Paul explains his role as a steward and servant of Christ in Ephesians 3:1-12. Read this passage carefully, identifying any and all linguistic artistry of the language. Take particular note of the key phrases, "fellow heirs" and "fellow members."

1. What was the mystery?_____
_____
_____
_____

2. Look up the Greek for "fellow heir" and "fellow member" and conduct a word study to fully understand these words._____
_____
_____
_____

3. Where are echoes in Scripture for these words? What meaning do the echoes contribute?____
_____
_____
_____
_____

4. How does your understanding of "fellow heir" and "fellow member" conflict with some traditional theology?_____
_____
_____
_____

5. In verse 6, what does it mean to be a minister?_____
_____
_____
_____

6. God will call all of us to these same roles of stewards and ministers if we allow it. What must we do to answer the call of becoming a steward of Christ and a minister for God's people?_____
_____
_____
_____
_____

Application Questions

1. A steward of God's household does not have to be a pastor of a church or a leader of a large group. Who are some stewards of God's people that you know who are caring for one person, or a small number of people? What makes them stewards? _____

   _____
   _____
   _____
   _____
   _____
   _____
   _____
   _____
   _____
   _____
   _____

2. Stewards are always servants, but are all servants stewards? Answer this question with specific examples from your life experiences. _____

   _____
   _____
   _____
   _____
   _____
   _____
   _____
   _____
   _____
   _____
   _____
   _____
   _____
   _____
   _____
   _____
   _____
   _____
   _____

Chapter 12 Quiz

1. What is an extended symbol?
   a. allusion
   b. ellipsis
   c. metaphor
   d. hyperbole

2. According to Scripture, "no man has seen God at any time."
   a. True
   b. False

3. Christ spoke for God because God was metaphorically in him.
   a. True
   b. False

4. Believers in Christ can speak for Christ, as Yeshua spoke for God, when they are metaphorically in Christ.
   a. True
   b. False

5. What was the mystery revealed in Colossians 1:27?
   a. those with faith in Christ have eternal life
   b. those who do not believe in Yeshua do not have eternal life
   c. God was in Christ reconciling the world unto Himself
   d. Christ is in those with faith in him

6. When you are "in Christ," this is a gift from God.
   a. True
   b. False

7. When Christ is "in you," you are walking as he walked.
   a. True
   b. False

8. According to Paul in Romans 8:10, all mankind is metaphorically dead because of sin.
   a. True
   b. False

9. What does the Greek word mean that has been translated "steward"?
   a. servant
   b. body of Christ
   c. manager of a household
   d. member of the body of Christ

10. To whom has it been granted to know the mysteries of the kingdom of heaven?
    a. believers in Yeshua
    b. all those who belong to God
    c. both Jews and Gentiles
    d. disciples of Yeshua

Made in the USA
Las Vegas, NV
06 October 2023

78678394R00081